Miniature Schnauzers

NIKKI MOUSTAKI

Miniature Schnauzers

Project Team
Editor: Adam Taliercio
Copy Editor: Stephanie Fornino
Indexer: Dianne L. Schneider
Design concept: Leah Lococo Ltd., Stephanie Krautheim
Design layout: Mary Ann Kahn

T.F.H. Publications
President/CEO: Glen S. Axelrod
Executive Vice President: Mark E. Johnson
Publisher: Christopher T. Reggio
Production Manager: Kathy Bontz

T.F.H. Publications, Inc.
One TFH Plaza
Third and Union Avenues
Neptune City, NJ 07753

Discovery Communications, Inc. Book Development Team:
Marjorie Kaplan, President and General Manager,
Animal Planet Media
Patrick Gates, President, Discovery Commerce
Elizabeth Bakacs, Vice President, Creative and Merchandising
Sue Perez-Jackson, Director, Licensing
Bridget Stoyko, Designer
Caitlin Erb, Licensing Manager

Printed and bound in China

08 09 10 11 12   1 3 5 7 9 8 6 4 2

Library of Congress Cataloging-in-Publication Data
Moustaki, Nikki, 1970-
  Miniature schnauzers / Nikki Moustaki
      p. cm. – (Animal planet pet care library)
  Includes index
  ISBN 978-0-7938-3702-1 (alk. paper)
  1. Miniature schnauzer. I. Title.
  SF429.M58M68 2008
  636.755–dc22
                            2008004385

This book has been published with the intent to provide accurate and authoritative information in regard to the subject matter within. While every reasonable precaution has been taken in preparation of this book, the author and publisher expressly disclaim responsibility for any errors, omissions, or adverse effects arising from the use or application of the information contained herein. The techniques and suggestions are used at the reader's discretion and are not to be considered a substitute for veterinary care. If you suspect a medical problem consult your veterinarian.

The Leader in Responsible Animal Care for Over 50 Years!®
www.tfh.com

Table of Contents

Chapter 1

Why I Adore My

Miniature Schnauzer

When I was in elementary school, a friend of mine owned the first Miniature Schnauzer I ever met, and once I got to know him I immediately became hooked on the breed. His name was Otto, and he was an incredible character. He was the first dog I knew who could do tricks, and I would spend an hour at a time having him give me his paw over and over—and he never faltered. His intelligence and patience amazed me, and I swore that someday I'd have a smart, affectionate, precious dog like Otto.

A Tale of Two Rescues

I finally got my first Miniature Schnauzer, Pepper, in 1996. He was a shelter dog who had been given up at 11 months old for excessive barking. Pepper came to me with a bad case of mange and a nervous temperament that would send him shivering into a corner if you merely tried to pet him.

I set out to learn everything I could about the breed and hopefully undo some of what Pepper's prior owners had done to him. I consulted trainers, breeders, groomers—anyone who knew anything about Mini Schnauzers. I learned a lot, but I learned more just by having Pepper in my life. I'm happy to report that he turned out to be my best friend, smart as a whip, and the most affectionate dog I've ever had.

My second Mini Schnauzer, Ozzie, came to me in 2002 at four years old, also a shelter dog. He arrived on a plane by himself, full of flea bite dermatitis and skin that was rotting and sloughing off. He had a dead look in his eyes, like the light inside that made him a dog had been snuffed out.

It took me six months to get his coat back to a healthy condition and another six to rouse his "inner puppy." Now Ozzie is laid back, a total chowhound, and is kind of "Lassie-like" in his manner—he likes to "tell" me

The Miniature Schnauzer makes a loving lapdog—and a protective watchdog.

when anything in the house is wrong, and he does an amazing job of it. I call him my "Mutant Mini" because he's much larger and taller than what the standard for a Mini Schnauzer calls for, and although he did lose some weight after I put him on a diet, his little potbelly seems to be permanent.

Taking the Good With the Not so Good

A Miniature Schnauzer can make an ideal pet, but no dog is completely perfect! In addition to all the wonderful ways a Mini can contribute to your life, there are other traits and quirks common to the breed that you need to be ready for when you acquire one.

Here are some of the joys of owning a Mini:

- He's protective although not an imposing figure.

- He's easy to transport.

- He makes a great lapdog.

- A Mini is a good first dog for someone learning about dog care and training.

- He's very expressive and will "tell" an owner what he wants.

- He's good with calm, gentle children (over the age of 10).

- A Mini sheds very little.

Talking up a Storm

Not only does the Mini like to bark at potential threats to his domain, he is the real "talker" of the three breeds of Schnauzers, able to have almost intelligible conversations with his owner. The range of the Mini's "talking" can go from low, growl-like grumbles to a yelping bawl that can sound alarming at first, although it usually just means that the dog is very excited. Strangers to the breed often believe that a chatty Mini is growling at them aggressively, so inform your visitors that your dog is just "talking" so that they don't become scared or put off.

Lady and the Tramp

Did you know that Tramp, Lady's scruffy suitor, is a Schnauzer mix? The 1955 Disney film *Lady and the Tramp* inspired thousands of people to inquire about Cocker Spaniels and Schnauzers, and it catapulted the breeds to the top of the AKC's registration list. The image of Lady slurping spaghetti with Tramp is etched in the minds of any fan of the film; how could you not adore those two loveable dogs?

And here are some of the challenges of owning a Mini that you should prepare for:

- Minis bark—a lot.

- They can be stubborn and likely will "play deaf" if they don't feel like listening to you.

- Mini Schnauzers can never be off leash in unfenced areas.

- They require regular grooming.

- Minis are particularly temperature sensitive and need a sweater in cold weather (although you may think that decking your Mini out in a sweater is one of the joys of owning him!).

- They have a tendency to try to be the alpha of the family "pack."

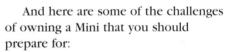

A Little Mini Schnauzer History

For the purposes of this book, I will use "Schnauzer" and "Mini" interchangeably to discuss the Miniature Schnauzer. Keep in mind, however, that there are two other types of Schnauzer: the Giant Schnauzer and the Standard Schnauzer, both of whom are distinct breeds, not two sizes of the same breed. The Miniature Schnauzer is the smallest of these three Schnauzer breeds.

As with many other dogs, the origins of the Mini Schnauzer are debatable, but the breed is said to have some Pomeranian, Affenpinscher, Poodle, and Miniature Pinscher in its background, along with the Standard Schnauzer, who provided the genetic blueprint for the Mini as well as the Giant.

What is certain is that this feisty dog has long been well loved for his exuberance, affection, and indomitable spirit. The early Mini Schnauzer was used in Germany as a farm ratter and vermin hunter. Eventually he also became treasured as a great watchdog. He became known as the Schnauzer because of the beard on his muzzle. (*Schnauzer* is the German word for "snout.") The breed has been depicted in artwork dating from as early as the turn of the 15th century.

The Mini was first exhibited as a breed distinct from the Standard Schnauzer in 1899. The breed is classified as a terrier but has no true terrier blood. Like terriers, though, the Mini is known to "go to ground"

The American Kennel Club first recognized the Mini Schnauzer in 1926.

to chase vermin (follow them underground to their lairs), which was his original purpose as a farm dog.

The Mini in the US
The first Mini Schnauzer litter in the United States was whelped in 1925 by a dam named Amsel. It is said that most champion Miniature Schnauzers owe some of their genetic code to Amsel.

The American Kennel Club (AKC) officially recognized the Mini Schnauzer in 1926. Both the AKC and the Canadian Kennel Club (CKC) consider the

What's a Schnoodle?

"Designer dogs," or deliberately crossbred dogs, have become very popular lately. The Poodle is at the root of most of these mixes—the "Doodle dogs," as they're called—and a Schnoodle is a Schnauzer/Poodle mix. This "mutt" happens to be quite adorable and usually has a combination of the good traits of each of the purebred parents—intelligence, a nonshedding coat, and fine watchdog skills.

Miniature Schnauzer a terrier, but in other countries he's classified in the non-sporting group. The Mini is currently the most popular of the three Schnauzer breeds in the US, with more than ten times the number of Minis registered in recent years than Giants and Standard Schnauzers combined.

General Appearance
The recognized Mini colors are black-and-silver, salt-and-pepper, and black. Minis can come in other colors such as silver, solid white, liver, and others, but these dogs can't be shown in conformation events. There is also a

Minis are active, affectionate dogs who love spending time with their owners.

can make wonderful pets.

The Miniature Schnauzer, according to the AKC standard, is a "robust, active dog of terrier type, resembling his larger cousin, the Standard Schnauzer." His coat is coarse, with a hard, wiry outercoat and a soft undercoat. The typical Schnauzer groom leaves a beard and long eyebrows that extend over the eye, as well as a skirt—these characteristics are all called "furnishings."

The Mini is square in proportion of body height to length and has a sturdy build. He is 12 to 14 inches (30.5 to 35.6 cm) in height at the shoulder according to the standard, but this range mainly applies to show dogs—a pet Mini Schnauzer can be larger or smaller than that. A healthy Mini usually weighs between 13 and 20 pounds (5.9 and 9.1 kg).

relatively new "parti-colored" Mini with sections of the coat that are different from the primary color. For example, the dog may have splotches of black or brown on a white body.

The following basic description represents the "ideal" Schnauzer that might participate in conformation dog shows, where judges evaluate dogs on their physical appearance. For the average companion Schnauzer, kept only as a pet, beauty standards need not be this strict. The most motley of Minis

Temperament and Personality

The Mini has personality in abundance. He's an expressive dog who loves having contact with his owner at all times and wants nothing more than to sit on her lap and be loved. He's not an aloof guy who's content to just laze by the fire—unless you're lazing by the fire with him. He can also be a fiercely

FAMILY-FRIENDLY TIP

Schnauzers and Kids: Are They a Good Match?

Dogs and kids go together like cookies and milk—as long as both the cookie and the milk behave themselves! A Schnauzer puppy raised with good-tempered, older kids is likely to become a wonderful member of the family. Children should learn to interact appropriately with dogs, and younger children, especially, need adult supervision with a Schnauzer at all times. This isn't a breed that's going to take well to being teased or bossed around roughly by anyone of any age.

protective watchdog, and although not many burglars may find this diminutive beast very daunting, at least his loud mouth will alert the family to any danger, real or imagined.

Activity Level

Mini Schnauzers are prone to obesity, so make sure that you put yours on a regular exercise program. Fortunately, these active little dogs love daily walks and a hardy game of tug in the yard. They are also great at playing fetch—because Minis were originally vermin hunters, they are still inclined

to chase and catch things. Your Mini is not likely to be a good jogging partner, however—he may love to run, but that kind of stamina is really more suited to a sporting breed.

Environment

The Mini is an incredibly adaptable fellow who can be as happy in a rural environment as he can in an urban apartment. Wherever he is, though, the Mini is meant to be a housedog, and he will never be content by himself in a yard or kennel all day. A Miniature Schnauzer needs the company of his humans.

Also keep in mind that Schnauzers are frequent barkers, and in a setting where your Mini will live in close proximity to neighbors, you have to work diligently with your puppy to curb a potential barking habit early.

Prey Drive

It's important for this breed to be on leash at all times when not indoors or in a fenced area. The Mini was bred to be a ratter, to hunt and kill vermin like many other terriers, and his prey drive is quite strong—he has a powerful urge to chase small moving objects, and this can land him in deep trouble. Keep this trait in mind if you have a small animal or bird as a pet.

Family Suitability

Generally speaking, Schnauzers have solid and good-natured temperaments and are well behaved when trained and cared for properly. A typical

12

Schnauzer loves the company of people. He is likely to make a good housedog and more often than not will get along with other pets—but keep an eye on any pet rodents you have in the house, or they may become your Mini's toys.

Every so often there will be a Schnauzer who is either shy or aggressive, so try to acquire your Mini from a reputable breeder, and if you can, see the parents before you take your puppy home. The traits exhibited by the parents are likely to manifest in your own dog as he grows up.

Trainability

Intelligent and a good problem solver, the Mini Schnauzer is highly trainable and both willing and able to learn complex behaviors if the rewards—usually in the form of treats or praise—are good enough. Of course, some Minis can also be obstinate and may pretend not to hear an owner's commands if there's something better to do than come when called.

This breed does very well in obedience trials and also excels in agility competitions, but it takes a patient owner to train a Schnauzer who might be more interested in barking at squirrels in the park than learning to do a long *down-stay*. Minis are definitely motivated by food, but some individuals find praise more motivating, and still others prefer toys and playtime. As you get to know your dog, you will find what works best for him.

All in all, the Miniature Schnauzer is the total package: He's smart, beautiful, small without being toyish, protective, affectionate, observant, and devoted. I bet you can't own just one!

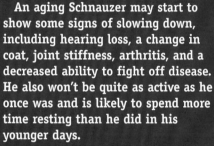

SENIOR DOG TIP

When is My Dog a Senior?

The age at which a dog becomes a senior depends on his size and breed. Small dogs tend to have longer life spans than larger ones—Miniature Schnauzers are generally considered senior citizens when they are about ten years old, although the aging process varies from dog to dog.

An aging Schnauzer may start to show some signs of slowing down, including hearing loss, a change in coat, joint stiffness, arthritis, and a decreased ability to fight off disease. He also won't be quite as active as he once was and is likely to spend more time resting than he did in his younger days.

A healthy senior dog can still have many good years ahead of him as long as he is well cared for. If your Mini is entering his golden years, ask your veterinarian about changing his diet to better meet a senior's nutritional needs, and make sure to keep up with regular health exams. (You may also want to schedule them more frequently, such as twice a year instead of annually.) Also remember that your older Schnauzer isn't as spry as he once was, and he may need help getting in and out of the car or his bed.

Chapter 2

The Stuff of Everyday Life

Dogs need supplies to keep them well cared for and happy, just as humans do. You probably wouldn't walk out of the house without brushing your hair or eating your cereal out of a clean bowl, and your Schnauzer needs the same consideration. This chapter will give you the rundown on what you need to make living with a Schnauzer much easier—for both of you.

Bed

Even if you allow your Schnauzer to sleep in your bed, he will still need a place of his own to lie down when you need him to stay out of the way or when he wants a nap. If you buy a good-quality bed from the start, you won't have to replace it as often, but expect to replace most beds every few years.

Your Schnauzer's bed should be large enough for him to curl up on or in. It should also be soft and comfy, and most importantly, durable and washable. Schnauzers tend to like bolster or donut beds (cushioned, usually rounded beds with raised edges), but a very soft cushion-type bed will do. Your Mini will also appreciate a small pillow.

Collars

Your Mini should wear a collar at all times when he's out of the house or has access to the yard but not when confined to his crate or when you're not supervising him. Without anyone there to keep an eye on him, his collar could catch on something and lead to injury or worse.

A Schnauzer doesn't need a fancy collar, but with a dog as smart-looking as this, why not? (Think rhinestones, bows, and bright colors!) However, even though your dog might have a wardrobe full of decorative collars, you should still invest in a more practical collar as well, especially for training purposes.

Flat Buckle Collar

A flat, nylon buckle collar is ideal for training purposes and is the basic collar that should contain your dog's ID and rabies tags. You will probably

Setting Up a Schedule

Dogs thrive on scheduling—they're like the type A boss who wants the meeting to start exactly on time and everything "just so," or else heads might roll.

Well, it's not quite that extreme with dogs, but they do love their schedules, and your Mini will hold you to his by jumping on the door at walk time, knocking around the food bowl at mealtime, or just by looking up at you with those Schnauzer "schnootzypoo" eyes that are so hard to resist.

Puppies especially require a rigorous schedule because they need to eliminate often. Feed your puppy as often as your veterinarian suggests (usually two or three times a day), and take him out to eliminate first thing in the morning and then every two to three hours until bedtime.

Your adult dog will need to eliminate at least three times a day: morning, afternoon, and nighttime—and he will also appreciate an extra walk or some playtime in the yard if you can provide it.

Keep a collar on your Mini whenever he's out of the house.

damage. However, if your dog pulls on the leash, he will definitely pull even harder with a harness on because the pressure caused by pulling is less uncomfortable than it is with a neck collar. There's a type of harness that has the leash clip at the chest rather than at the shoulders, giving you a little more control of the dog—when he pulls, he gets turned around.

Head Halter

If your Schnauzer is having a hard time learning to walk well on a leash, you may want to fit him with a head halter. This product fits snugly over your dog's head and muzzle and forces him to turn his head to the side when he pulls. Eventually, he will realize that pulling isn't as much fun as being on the straight and narrow.

Some dogs have a poor reaction to the head halter initially, but you can avoid this by offering treats and putting the halter on your dog for a few minutes at a time to get him used to the sensation of having something on his head.

Crate

A crate, also called a kennel, is a safe place where your Schnauzer can go to escape all of the household activity and have a nice nap. It's also a place where you can put him when you leave the house or just need him out of the way for a little while.

need two of these collars: one for your dog as a puppy and an adjustable one for when he gets older. The collar should fit snugly, but you should also be able to easily fit two fingers between the collar and your dog's skin. Don't let the collar get too tight as your dog grows.

A flat or rolled leather collar is also a good choice for your dog's basic collar, but leather can begin to smell if it gets wet frequently. Nylon, on the other hand, is washable and comes in a variety of colors and patterns, although leather is a little more fashionable.

Harness

Many people like to walk smaller dogs with a body harness, which is advisable—some evidence shows that a small dog who pulls consistently on a neck collar can develop tracheal

Doggie Day Care and Dog Walkers

Schnauzers are small dogs with small bladders. A Schnauzer in his prime can wait several hours to take a potty break (although ideally, he shouldn't have to), but a puppy, adolescent, or senior isn't going to be able to "hold it" for that long.

Housetrained dogs do not want to have "accidents." Believe it or not, most housetrained dogs who eliminate in the house because they are desperate feel upset or badly about it. If you work all day and are unable to take your dog out to eliminate every few hours or so, consider sending him to day care or hiring a dog walker to take him out when you aren't around. In addition to preventing household accidents, dog walkers and day care facilities also give your dog some much-needed exercise. Research the walker or day care carefully, however, and try to talk to people who already use the service to find out if the dogs are treated kindly.

The crate never should be used as punishment, nor is it a "cage" in the usual sense. The crate is designed to safely contain a dog when he needs some downtime, when you're not home, or when you're traveling. Even if you're not going to use the crate every day, you should get him used to it so that he's comfortable there if you need to take him on a long car ride or board him, or if you have a visitor who's afraid of or allergic to dogs.

When purchasing a crate, buy a crate pad that fits the bottom of it. Crate pads are usually made of an acrylic, fleecy material. You can also use a flat dog bed or even an old blanket or towels to make the crate more comfortable.

Crate Types

There are three basic types of crates you can use: plastic, wire, and decorator.

Plastic

Crates made of molded plastic are durable, lightweight, and easy to clean, and most are airline-approved, making them ideal for traveling. Plastic crates are also dark inside, which gives the dog a sense of security.

Wire

Wire crates allow for good ventilation, give the dog a great view of his surroundings, and fold down for easy storage and transportation, but they are not airline-approved. Most manufacturers of wire crates also make fabric crate covers.

Decorator

Decorator crates come in a variety of materials, including wicker and wood,

If you make your Mini's crate a comfortable, safe place, he'll learn to love spending time there.

and are designed to fit nicely into any decor. These types of crates are better for a dog who is already crate trained and used to confinement.

Crate Size
Buy a crate that's the right size for your dog. He should be able to stand up and turn around comfortably, but the crate is not a condo, so there should not be room inside for food and a place to potty. The only things inside the crate should be a bed, your dog, and some safe toys, unless you have to confine him for more than a couple of hours, in which case there should also be a water source available.

Exercise Pen
An exercise pen is a series of gates locked together to form a barrier that confines your dog to a safe, circular area either inside the house or outdoors. Most ex-pens are expandable, and you can buy as many sections of the gate as you need to create an exercise area suitable for your dog. For a Schnauzer, make sure that the panels are at least 2 feet (.6 m) high to prevent him from climbing or jumping out.

If your dog's primary confinement area inside the house is an ex-pen, make it large enough to include a crate and an area at the opposite end where the dog can eliminate. Place toys and a water dish inside the pen and a soft bed inside the crate. Also, make sure that your dog isn't wearing a collar when he's inside, to prevent any potential choking hazards.

Food and Water Bowls
The pet marketplace has grown so significantly in the past several years that it's not unusual to see dog bowls that look like pieces of art made for royalty and others that don't even look like dog bowls at all. Your choices of materials, colors, and patterns are endless.

Food Bowls
The following are some different types of food bowls. They each have their advantages and disadvantages; what you end up purchasing is up to you—and your dog, of course. Whichever type of food bowl you choose, be sure to wash it with warm, soapy water after each meal.

Ceramic

Ceramic bowls are often designed with home decor in mind, but the glaze can craze and crack, and a ceramic bowl is much more likely to break during regular cleaning than a plastic or metal bowl. On the other hand, it is awfully nice to have a pretty ceramic bowl in the house, even if you have to replace it every few years.

Plastic

Plastic bowls are fine for starters, but they can scratch easily, and bacteria will grow in the crevices if you don't disinfect them thoroughly and frequently. If you do choose plastic, invest in good-quality bowls that you can put in the dishwasher.

Stainless Steel

Stainless steel bowls will last for your dog's entire life, are lightweight, dishwasher-safe, and come in all shapes and sizes. Schnauzer puppies will need smaller bowls at first but will graduate to larger bowls when they get older.

Water Bowls

Your dog's water bowl should be bottom-heavy, with a nonskid surface underneath to prevent it from sliding around the floor

Make sure that your Mini always has access to fresh, clean water.

as he drinks. Fill the bowl with fresh water at least twice a day, and keep water available for him at all times.

A drinking fountain-type bowl is also a nice option for any dog. This gadget has a small motor that circulates the water through a carbon filter, keeping it fresh and drinkable.

Whatever type of water bowl you choose to provide, clean it every day to prevent a buildup of bacteria.

If your dog spends any time outside, his outdoor play and potty area should contain a bowl of fresh water at all times. Alternatively, you can purchase a water dispenser that attaches to your garden hose to provide your Schnauzer with fresh water all the time—most large pet stores and online retailers carry this item. In the winter, water in a dish left outdoors will freeze, but your Mini shouldn't spend much time outside in the cold weather anyway.

Gate

Most trained adult Schnauzers are well behaved enough to have access to the entire house or at least most of it. However, if you don't want your dog—especially a puppy or an incontinent senior—to get into certain areas of

FAMILY-FRIENDLY TIP

Should Children Care for the Family Dog?

Responsible, compassionate kids and dogs are great together, but rowdy teens and rough toddlers aren't good housemates for many dogs. Also, some Minis can become set in their ways and may not be able to tolerate young kids as they get older.

No child, not even a teenager, should be solely responsible for the care of a Schnauzer. Of course, you can include aspects of caring for the dog into a child's list of chores, but please supervise feeding, watering, and grooming tasks to make sure that they're done right—or that they're done at all!

Identification

Your dog should have ID on him at all times. Thousands of dogs go missing each year, and many remain lost because of their lack of identification. Even if you think that your yard is escape-proof, your dog should be wearing a collar with ID tags that have his name and your phone number engraved on them.

Microchipping

If you lose your dog and his collar is torn off or removed (which happens more often than you'd think), he will need some permanent identification to find his way back home. Your veterinarian can inject a small microchip, about the size of a grain of rice, between your Schnauzer's shoulder blades. This chip has a number that will be registered to you and serves as a permanent way to identify your dog.

your home, use a baby gate to prevent him from roaming where you don't want him to go.

Baby gates are either tension mounted or installed in a doorway. Get a gate that is at least 24 to 36 inches (.6 to .9 m) high, and invest in a high-quality gate from the start—the less expensive models tend to break more easily.

Proper identification makes recovering your dog much more likely if he ever becomes lost.

Licensing Your Schnauzer

Most states and municipalities require that all dogs get rabies vaccinations each year. Usually, your veterinarian will license your dog at the same time and give you a tag to put on his collar. You can also use this tag as a form of identification because the number on the tag is unique to your dog and is registered with the state or town. If your dog is neutered or spayed, the license is usually very inexpensive, and the fees often go to help local shelters. If you choose not to fix your dog, the license costs a little more but not much. Licensing a service or working dog is usually free.

Most veterinarians and shelters have a scanner that can read the chip, much like the scanner at the supermarket reads a bar code. Insertion of the chip is not painful and won't cause an allergic reaction.

Leash

Use a 4- or 6-foot (1.2- or 1.8-m) leash while you're training your dog to walk nicely on the lead. (Because Mini Schnauzers are such small dogs, a 6-foot [1.8-m] leash may be the most practical.) You'll also need a 25-foot (7.6-m) cotton leash to use in the park or anywhere else you'll need to "reel in" your dog if he's not paying attention or has a tendency to run off. (Most Schnauzers are pretty easily distracted.) The long line is great for teaching the *come* command, as well as many other obedience commands.

Toys

Schnauzers love chewing and tearing up toys. Because of their history as vermin hunters, they adore squeaky toys that they can "kill" like they'd kill rodents. Any toy that includes food in some way is also good for this breed. Don't let your Schnauzer get too carried away with squeaky toys, however—many dogs find a way to remove the squeaker

Minis love squeaky toys, which remind them of the rodents their ancestors used to hunt.

Older Rescued Schnauzers

One of the nicest things you can do is adopt an older dog from a rescue or shelter. Many owners give up their Schnauzers for adoption, some because of behavior issues but most because the owner was moving, had a new baby, or didn't want the dog for some other reason having nothing to do with the pet's lovability.

When bringing home an adult rescue dog, don't expect too much of him at first. Give him time to get to know your home and family. Show him where to go potty and where to find his food, water, and bed. If he has an accident, simply clean it up and show him again where he should go. Refrain from any form of scolding. Give him a variety of toys and a bed placed in a quiet location, such as inside his crate.

Older Schnauzers who were socialized correctly tend to be mellower than some other breeds and will adjust well to a new home if provided with the proper introduction.

and may swallow it, which can pose a choking hazard.

Puppies in particular need "teething toys" to keep them away from your valuables. Some of the companies that make hard rubber toys are also making softer toys especially designed for a puppy's teeth and gums. Also, always buy appropriately sized toys—it might be fun to watch your small Schnauzer try to eat a dinosaur bone-sized chew, but it might become frustrating for him. On the other hand, toys that are made for tiny dogs may pose a choking hazard for your Mini.

Here's a list of toys that your Schnauzer will like.

- hard rubber toys that you can stuff with treats and food
- plush squeaky toys (you may have to remove the squeaker if your Mini has a tendency to remove it himself)
- rope and tugging toys
- rubber squeaky toys (take them away them once they become worn)
- tennis balls of varying sizes
- treat-dispensing toys

If you have a shopping fixation, there are a lot of other goodies you can buy for your Schnauzer: everything from designer dog beds to collars and clothes to show off his fashion sense. But remember, Schnauzers don't need these things to be happy. Just having the basics is enough—oh, and plenty of squeaky toys!

Chapter 3

Good Eating

Schnauzers are generally active dogs who require a high-quality diet to function properly. However, even a couch potato Schnauzer needs a premium diet to prevent premature aging, coat problems, and serious health issues. Poor nutrition can also eventually lead to problem behaviors.

Food Basics

Use the highest-quality food available for your Schnauzer's staple diet, ideally one that's considered "super premium." Super premium foods often contain organic ingredients and human-grade supplements. Even the "premium" foods often fall short of being adequate for your dog's ongoing health.

Here is a rundown of the basic components of a high-quality canine diet, but you should discuss which type of food is best for your Mini with your vet.

Carbohydrates

Low-carb diets are prevalent among humans trying to lose weight, but carbohydrates should make up about 50 percent of your dog's food. Corn, soy, rice, potato, or wheat are the primary carbs in most dog foods, and these are fine if they come from good-quality crops, but many dog food companies use cheap feed that adds little or no nutritional value to the product. If your dog becomes bloated or gassy, or if he develops allergies, filler in his diet may be to blame.

Fats

Fats promote coat, skin, kidney, and connective tissue health. They also make food tastier and are often added to kibble at the end of the extrusion process. An active, fit dog needs some

fats in his diet; diets that are low in fat are intended only for overweight and senior dogs.

You can add beneficial fats to your dog's diet with a supplement of omega fatty acid, but consult your vet before offering any dietary supplements to your pet.

Proteins

A good-quality animal protein should be the first ingredient in your dog's food, and the ideal food has another animal-based ingredient as its second or third ingredient as well. Proteins that come from corn or rice meal aren't as digestible for dogs as those from a meat source and are considered filler.

High-protein diets are recommended for puppies and very active dogs, but too much protein cam cause kidney issues for the average dog.

Offer your Mini the highest-quality food available.

Vitamins and Minerals

As with humans, dogs need vitamins and minerals to function. High-quality dog food usually contains the right amount of vitamins and minerals to keep your dog fit, but you may want to supplement the food with a product recommended by your veterinarian.

Water

Water is the basis for life, and your Schnauzer should have plenty of it available at all times. Active dogs who play outside in warm weather can become dehydrated, so always carry a water bottle and portable bowl when you're enjoying some summer fun. When you're housetraining your dog, many trainers recommend removing the water dish after he has eaten and drunk his fill so that he can't keep filling up on water and won't have to potty as often. This is generally okay, but you want to work up to keeping the dish available all the time.

Reading Food Labels

There are regulations governing what a dog food manufacturer can and cannot claim on a dog food label. Reading food labels isn't as easy as it may seem, but if you know how to read them, you'll know exactly what you're feeding to your dog. Here's a short tutorial on what to look for on dog food labels.

Product Name

If the dog food's name has an ingredient in its title, it must contain 95 percent of that type of food before water is added, and then it still has to contain at least 70 percent of the named ingredient. For example, "Liver for Schnauzers" Dog Food (a make-believe brand) must be 70 percent liver *after* water is added. If the food were

Supplements

Every veterinarian, groomer, trainer, breeder, and dog expert will have a different opinion on the controversial subject of canine dietary supplements, but don't supplement your dog's diet without getting some advice from your vet on the subject. Too much of a good thing isn't always beneficial—you can throw your dog's system out of whack and cause health problems. However, if you have a dog who has been ill or who is especially active, he may need some additional nutrients to keep him healthy.

You can find canine supplements online or at your local independent pet retailer. Some of the supplements make various health claims, such as improving joint health or skin condition, but they may or may not actually work. Some human-grade supplements, like green foods, kelp, flaxseed oil, fish oils, and some holistic supplements can be added to your dog's diet with no adverse effects.

Good Eating

Read food labels carefully to ensure that your Mini's food provides proper nutrition.

called "Liver and Fish for Schnauzers," it would still have to be 70 percent liver and fish after water was added, but it also must contain more liver than fish.

"Dinner"

If the name of the product has "dinner" in it (or "formula," "nuggets," "entrée," or "platter")—for example, "Fish Dinner for Schnauzers," the food must be at least 25 percent fish. Fish, in this case, will not be the first ingredient but probably the third, fourth, or fifth. If the name of the food was "Fish and Kidney Dinner for Schnauzers," both food items would have to add up to 25 percent of the meal, but at least 3 percent of that would have to be kidney.

"With"

If a product claims that it contains something "with" the main ingredient—for example, "Venison and Lamb Dinner for Schnauzers With Bacon," the bacon part of the meal only has to make up 3 percent of the product. If there are two items after the word "with," each of those ingredients has to compose 3 percent of the product separately.

"Flavor"

A dog food "flavored" with an ingredient doesn't have to include a percentage of that flavor in the meal. The company might add broth, by-products, whey, or chemicals to get that flavor.

Meat Source

The first ingredient on a dog food label should be a meat source such as lamb, beef, chicken, fish, venison, duck, and so forth. Try not to buy anything that lists "animal by-products" as one of the first ingredients. This means that the food may contain indigestible proteins, hair, hide, or even diseased animal parts.

Fillers

Fillers include rice hulls, corn, wheat, oatmeal, and even some food items that are good for humans but aren't necessarily good for dogs. Poor-quality fillers, like corn, aren't digestible and shouldn't be in your dog's food, or should at least be fifth or lower on the list of ingredients.

Most dog foods contain fillers, but premium foods will contain better-quality fillers. Poor-quality foods might have fillers that came from sweeping the processing plant's floors or from grains that were too substandard to feed to livestock.

Preservatives

Artificial preservatives aren't good for humans, and they certainly aren't good for dogs, either; they can cause hair loss, cancer, allergies, kidney problems, and many other health issues. Artificial preservatives include ethoxyquin, butylated hydroxytoluene (BHT), and butylated hydroxyanisole (BHA), and you should avoid foods that list these among their ingredients. Natural preservatives such as tocopherols (vitamin E) and ascorbic acid (vitamin C) are much safer for your dog.

A meat source (not a meat by-product) should be the first ingredient in your Schnauzer's food.

Commercial Foods

The easiest foods to give your Schnauzer are commercial dog foods: Just open a can, a bag, or both, and dole out the correct portions (usually listed on the label). If you choose to give your dog a commercial food, remember to only purchase a super premium food, ideally a brand recommended by your veterinarian or breeder.

When choosing a commercially made dog food, consider the following:

- The foremost requirement for a dog food is that your dog likes it and will eat it. The brand might be the best, healthiest food in the world, but there's no point in offering it if your dog is just going to snub it.

FAMILY-FRIENDLY TIP

Feeding Time

Mealtime is one of the highlights of your Schnauzer's day, so it's fun to get the kids involved. Supervise your children and show them how to mix the food, but always have an adult offer the bowl to the dog. Your child should not be the sole provider of food for the dog—adults in the household must regulate how much he is eating on a daily basis. Also, make sure that children in your household know to leave the dog alone as he eats and understand that they only should remove the bowl when the dog has finished eating.

- The brand should have viable, usable nutrients. (The more premium the food, the more viable the nutrients.)

- Is your dog thriving on the food? If the food is causing gas and intestinal problems, allergies (including itching and hair loss), or other symptoms, change his diet.

- Choose the right "formula." There are formulas for puppies, active dogs, less active dogs, and seniors. Use the one best suited for your pet and his lifestyle.

Dry Food (Kibble)

Dry dog food is easy to feed, and its crunchy texture helps keep your dog's teeth clean. Kibble usually contains about ten percent moisture, so you're getting about 90 percent actual food. If you give your dog dry food, choose baked kibble over extruded because it loses far fewer nutrients during the heating process. If your dog is a picky eater, you can mix kibble with a spoonful of wet food and a little bit of water to make it more palatable.

Semi-Moist Food

Semi-moist dog foods contain about 40 percent moisture, so you're getting about 60 percent actual food for your buck. Many of the commercial versions are full of artificial ingredients and sugars, but premium products come in organic and all-natural formulas. This type of food is good for dogs who won't eat kibble or who have dental problems. Semi-moist dog food can also make a great between-meal snack or treat.

Canned Food

Canned dog food is about 75 percent moisture, so you're basically paying for a can of water—but it's yummy water! Canned dog foods can't be more than 78 percent water by law, but if the labels say "stew" or "with gravy," they can be up to nearly 88 percent water. Premium brands have better ingredients, so they provide more nutrition even though they are still mostly water.

Table Manners

All dogs should have good table manners. First, you must teach your Schnauzer to sit before you put down his food dish or before he gets a treat. Sitting is the doggy equivalent of saying "please" and should be in your dog's vocabulary of behaviors. (For information on how to teach *sit*, see Chapter 6.)

Also, always feed your Schnauzer after you eat your meal—the leader of the pack always eats first. Although your Schnauzer may behave like he's starving while he waits and give you those "schnootzypoo" eyes, he is programmed to accept this, and he'll be just fine.

Finally, make sure that your dog isn't doing any "resource guarding": growling if you come near him while he's eating or showing his teeth or snapping at you when you try to remove his bowl before he's done. These are very serious behaviors that you must address as soon as they appear.

Good Eating

Noncommercial Diets

Home-cooked or raw noncommercial diets are also options for some Schnauzer owners, and many people who feed their dogs these diets swear by them. Both of these diets can be costly and time consuming, but they are worth it for people who want to go this route.

Never feed a cooked or raw diet in addition to kibble, however—these meals digest differently, and you'll give your dog a tummy ache (or worse) if you combine them with a commercial food. Consult your veterinarian before embarking on a new diet plan for your Schnauzer.

Home-Cooked Diet

Home-cooked diets are savory and delicious, and most Schnauzers enjoy them more than kibble or canned foods. Also, a home-cooked diet doesn't contain preservatives. This diet includes mostly human-grade foods, like low-fat cuts of meat, deboned chicken, fish, fruits and veggies, healthy grains, yogurt, and human-grade supplements. Dog owners who offer this type of diet say that their dogs have more energy, shed less, and are leaner.

The real issue with this diet is time and feasibility because you have to cook each of your dog's meals yourself. You can make a large amount once a week and freeze the food in portions if that's more convenient, but do some research on what it takes to prepare these meals, and determine whether you would be willing or able to cook your dog's meals at home.

Raw Diet

The raw diet comprises raw meats, often with the bones still attached, and can be bought in a store or made at home. The homemade version is

Feeding Schedule for Each Phase of Your Schnauzer's Life

	Puppies (2 to 6 months)	Adolescents (6 to 18 months)	Active Adults (18 months to 6+ years)	Sedentary Adults (3 to 7+ years)	Seniors (9+ years)
Times per Day	2-3	2	2	1-2	1-2
Best Food	Puppy formula (protein less than 25%)	Active formula	Adult formula	Adult or senior formula (protein less than 22%)	Senior formula

Along with a proper diet, regular exercise will help keep your Schnauzer from becoming obese.

known as the BARF (Bones and Raw Food) diet and has specific guidelines about how it should be served. Meat alone isn't nutritionally balanced for dogs, so they need the bones as well. However, you should never feed your dog cooked bones because they can splinter and cause punctures in the digestive tract. Usually, BARF diets include the wings, back, and neck of the chicken because these bones don't splinter when they're raw. You can also include organ meats, eggs, some veggies, and apple cider vinegar as part of a raw diet. Research this feeding method carefully and ask your veterinarian for advice before you try it on your dog.

Treats

There's not a Schnauzer out there who doesn't appreciate a good treat. Treats not only provide a dog with a lot of pleasure, but they're also a fundamental part of the training process.

Some treats are actually very nutritious, while others are just "junk food." The better quality treats are available at boutique pet stores, although many of the larger stores are getting wise to the need for better, healthier treats. If your dog is a little round in the middle and could benefit from a diet, you can find low-fat and low-calorie treats as well as treats with added nutritional supplements. Remember not to use "people" food as treats—you may make your dog ill that way.

Feeding Schedules

Schnauzers do well on two meals a day rather than the "free feeding" method (allowing the dog to have food at will), which can lead to obesity and may damage the dog's digestive tract. Your veterinarian can tell you how much to feed your dog, or you can feed him according to the dog food label.

Obesity

Schnauzers have a tendency to become porky easily, so it's essential to regulate the amount of food your dog receives and give him adequate exercise. Even though your Schnauzer might look up at you with those cute eyes that say "Help me, I'm *starving*," he's really not. There's nothing wrong with between-meal snacks, but a little goes a long way.

Side Effects of Obesity

Overweight dogs can suffer from the same debilitating conditions as overweight humans, such as diabetes, joint problems, heart issues, and immune system dysfunction. Thinner dogs live significantly longer and don't age as quickly as heavier dogs. An extra snack or two a day might be fun for your dog, but it isn't going to make his life better. Actually, those extra calories could eventually kill him.

How to Tell if Your Schnauzer Is Obese

The "appropriate" weight for Schnauzers is only a median range for each gender and does not account for your individual dog's body type or activity level. Your veterinarian will be able to tell you the weight that's appropriate for your individual dog.

Don't let the scale determine whether to put your Schnauzer on a diet and exercise program. Instead, look closely at your dog in the following ways:

A Mini with a sedentary lifestyle is more likely to become overweight.

1. **Feel his ribs.** If you can feel them and the spaces between them and there's not a layer of fat over them, then your dog is probably a good weight for his body type. If you can see his ribs well, he's too thin.

2. **Look at your Schnauzer from above.** He should have a waist. If he looks more like a sausage, he needs to lose a few pounds (kg).

3. **Look at your dog from the side.** His stomach should tuck upward as his abdomen reaches his haunches. If he's more barrel shaped, it's time for a diet.

What to Do if Your Schnauzer Is Obese

There are low-calorie and diet foods on the market that make it easy to put your dog on a weight-loss program. Talk to your veterinarian about all of your options, which may include changing food brands, switching to a senior formula, or simply cutting back on portions. Be careful not to let your dog lose too much weight too quickly, however. For most dogs, losing one percent of body weight per week is safe, but more than that can be dangerous, so don't put your dog on a crash diet.

You can also change the way you feed your pudgy pup. For example, rather than just pouring food in his bowl, stuff his portions into a hard rubber toy and make him work for them, or scatter some of his food in the yard and have him hunt for his meal. Also, use his regular mealtime kibble for treats rather than adding additional treats to his diet.

SENIOR DOG TIP

Feeding Your Senior

Senior dogs don't need as many calories as active adults do. Schnauzers are considered seniors when they're about eight or nine years old, and they may need a diet change as they age. Low-calorie treats like carrots, green beans, and freeze-dried chicken are better choices than fatty or sugary commercial treats or table foods.

Senior dogs also need more exercise, even though they don't move as quickly anymore. Try not to let your dog become a couch potato.

Exercise is critical for weight loss as well, and an exercise program for your dog doesn't have to be complicated. A vigorous game of fetch in the yard is great exercise for your dog, as are extended walks and romps in the dog park. (And you'll be getting some extra exercise yourself!)

Taking the time to feed your Schnauzer correctly and providing him with enough proper exercise goes a long way toward keeping him healthy and extending his life. Try not to confuse food with love—food is sustenance. Belly rubs are love.

Good Eating

Chapter 4

Looking Good

Properly groomed Schnauzers shed extremely little, which makes them great pets for people with allergies and for those who don't want "hair bunnies" under the furniture. Of course, it's still important to keep up with your grooming chores because the Mini's coat can become matted. Also, even though he isn't a "smelly" dog, like any other pet he can become malodorous when not bathed or brushed for a while.

Mini Schnauzers have a specific grooming style that you can maintain for your dog, or you can choose to keep grooming simple and opt for a shorter puppy cut instead, keeping only the typical Schnauzer beard and eyebrows. I have even shaved my dogs from head to toe in the summertime, but I must admit that they don't look much like Schnauzers in that case!

The Benefits of Grooming

In addition to keeping a dog's coat, skin, teeth, ears, eyes, and nails clean and healthy, proper grooming can help prevent health problems as well. It gives the owner an opportunity to notice if there are any issues arising, such as dental problems, tumors, or eye conditions. You can't help but look closely at your dog while you're grooming him, and if you do it regularly enough, any physical changes in your dog will be obvious. Grooming is also a fantastic way for Schnauzers and their owners to bond.

Getting Your Dog Used to Grooming

Dogs who require complicated grooming or trips to the salon won't enjoy their grooming routine without being socialized to it at an early age, so start getting your puppy used to grooming as soon as you bring him home. You can brush him gently—offering treats while doing so—for as little as two minutes a day to start. You just want him to get used to feeling the brush and comb on his skin.

After a few weeks, you can add the noise of the clipper or the blow dryer. Remember, you're just getting him used to the feelings and sounds of grooming, not actually clipping him. Give him treats to make him more comfortable, but stop everything if he becomes scared.

A well-groomed Mini Schnauzer is a sight to behold!

FAMILY-FRIENDLY TIP

Children and Grooming

Although a young child can help in the grooming process, do not allow her to be solely responsible for your dog's grooming. Supervise grooming sessions to make sure that the child is being gentle and grooming the dog properly. Your dog should associate grooming with good feelings, not pain. Teach your child how to be gentle when grooming and to always brush with the grain of the coat. Do not allow your child to clean your Schnauzer's ears or eyes or to trim his nails.

Keep grooming sessions short, especially if you're working on a dog who isn't used to this kind of attention. Reward him with treats for staying still and allowing you to touch his feet, muzzle, and ears. Don't force any kind of close interaction. If your dog doesn't like having his feet touched, for example, try touching the top of one foot for one second and then offering a treat. Then, touch the foot for two seconds and offer a treat, and so on. Work your way up to holding his foot and inspecting his pads, the area in between the pads, and the nails, but take it slowly. Maintaining a slow pace is especially important with a puppy less than 20 weeks of age, when any type of trauma may affect the way he perceives the world for the rest of his life.

Grooming Supplies

Before you can groom your dog, you need to have all the tools necessary to do the job. Here is a quick rundown of the grooming supplies you may need:

- after-bath spray (optional)
- dog conditioner (optional)
- dog shampoo
- dog toothpaste and toothbrush
- guillotine-style nail clippers (or electric, if you're experienced with them)
- natural bristle brush and/or nylon bristle brush
- rubber-backed pin brush
- sharp-toothed comb
- slicker brush (for a show coat only)
- stripping knives (for a show coat only)
- styptic powder or cornstarch
- washcloths
- wide-toothed comb

Coat Care

The Mini Schnauzer has a double coat—a hard, wiry outercoat and a soft, dense undercoat. The outercoat serves to keep the dog clean, while the undercoat keeps him warm. This isn't a high-maintenance coat like you'd have with an Afghan Hound, but it's not low maintenance like you'd have

39

Looking Good

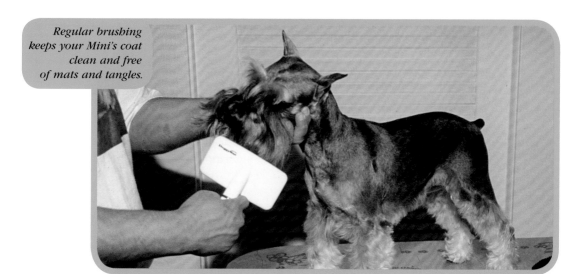

Regular brushing keeps your Mini's coat clean and free of mats and tangles.

with a Smooth Fox Terrier, either; it's somewhere in between.

The Schnauzer's coat usually needs professional grooming for its upkeep. People who show their Schnauzers make a great effort to keep their dogs' coats perfectly groomed, but even if you have no intention of showing your dog, there's a certain "Schnauzer look" that you're probably going to want to maintain.

Of course, you can choose to groom your dog yourself rather than get professional help, but you must learn how to do it properly and use the necessary tools—and that's not as easy as it looks!

Pet Groom or Show Groom?

You have two basic but quite different options as to how to groom your Mini: the shorter, more manageable pet groom; or the show groom, which your dog must have if you want to show him. The show-style groom is much more time consuming and requires that the groomer have experience with this breed. (Pretty much any groomer can do the pet style groom.)

The Pet Groom

The pet groom is probably what you're going to have done to your Schnauzer. You have two basic options: a clipped-down cut or a puppy cut. The clipped look makes the Mini look exactly like his show counterparts but with shorter, less coarse hair on the back and sides. You can also clip the entire dog, leaving just the hair on the face. Or you can choose a puppy cut, which is when the hair on the entire body is clipped uniformly, usually about 1 or 2 inches (2.5 or 5.1 cm) long.

If you're going to do a clipped-down cut, you will have to take your Schnauzer to the groomer about every 8 to 12 weeks. You can extend the time between visits by trimming the hair around the

and the distinctiveness of his markings. However, if you don't know how to groom your dog for a show, *you must have someone show you how to do it (or hire a professional groomer).* This isn't something you're going to learn how to do well from a book. You have to find a mentor who is willing to show you exactly what to do, and then you have to learn through trial and error on your own dog. Don't expect that just any groomer will know how to groom your Mini the way the show groomers do it, either—it's time consuming, and it's not a typical request.

Creating a show-quality coat requires a process called "stripping." When stripping the coat, the groomer pulls out dead or dying coarse hairs and undercoat from the root, allowing new hairs to grow. Stripping can be done by hand or by using a stripping knife. On a show Schnauzer, the face and furnishings (the hair on the legs) are stripped, clipped, or cut into an exaggerated style. Minis look amazing in a show groom, but it's difficult at best for a pet owner to maintain. You can, however, maintain a modified

face and the feet yourself with a pair of sharp scissors, but be careful.

I don't recommend that you try to save some money by clipping your dog yourself. If you're not trained with the electric clippers, you can make your dog look really terrible—or accidentally hurt him.

The Show Groom

A Mini with a show groom is a beautiful creature. All of his best features are accentuated: the rectangular shape of his head, the squareness of his body,

> ## The Grooming Table
> A professional pet groomer uses a grooming table to lift a dog up off the floor so that she doesn't have to bend over to work on him. The dog wears a special slip collar that attaches to a line on the grooming table to prevent him from jumping off. You don't need your own grooming table to work on your Schnauzer, however; if bending over hurts your back, you can brush him on your bed or couch.

version of the show coat if you learn to strip the hair properly.

Brushing Your Schnauzer

Brushing your Schnauzer is a good way to keep his coat and skin healthy. It also stimulates the hair follicles and helps the natural oils from his skin make the coat more water resistant. Brushing also helps remove debris and dirt from the Schnauzer's coat. In general, he will require brushing every other day or so, or more if he spends time outside playing in places where his coat can pick up dirt or burrs.

Use a soft bristle brush on a young dog to get him used to grooming. (You can also use this brush on a clipped dog.) Use a pin brush if your dog has thicker hair; if you keep him in a show coat, use a slicker brush on his legs.

A quick once-over every day just after you come in from a walk will keep your Mini's coat in really good shape. If you let it get too long and it becomes matted, you will have no choice but to shave him down.

How to Brush Your Schnauzer

Brushing involves more than just running the brush over the dog's back and calling it a day! Brush your dog's sides, belly, legs, chest, and neck to avoid matting. Brush in the direction of the coat, not against it. Don't go near the nose or eyes when you brush because these areas are sensitive. Use a metal comb to keep the eyebrows and beard in good order and to prevent the beard from matting. Have some treats on hand, and praise your dog liberally for any compliance, no matter how small.

Bathing Your Schnauzer

Your Schnauzer will probably only need a bath about once every three months or longer, but you can bathe him more frequently if he gets especially stinky or if you're taking him to your mother-in-law's house for Thanksgiving. Bathing a Schnauzer too often can dry out his skin, however, so don't overdo it.

How to Bathe Your Schnauzer Indoors

Your first concern when bathing your Mini is where you're going to give him the bath. The family bathtub will work,

Towel dry your Schnauzer after his bath.

but if your Mini is small enough, you can use the kitchen sink. If you use the bathtub, place a rubber mat or a towel on the floor of the tub so that it isn't slippery, and line the bathroom floor with towels so that it remains dry.

Have your shampoo bottle open and towels nearby before you begin. Use a shampoo that does not irritate the eyes and that is made specifically for dogs, not humans, because dogs need a different pH balance and human shampoos can dry their skin. There are even bar soaps made for dogs these days, but don't use human bar soap. If you like, you can also use a dog-specific conditioner to make your dog's coat shiny and smell clean.

Start the bath by wetting your dog to the skin with lukewarm water—not too hot, not too cold. You can purchase a shower hose attachment (available at any pet store or through an online retailer) so that rinsing is easier. If you don't have one, use a large plastic measuring cup with a handle to wet and rinse the dog.

The Schnauzer's coat is water resistant, especially if it's stripped rather than clipped, so rub your dog all over with your hands to soak in the water. Tilt his head back when you wet it so that the water doesn't get into his eyes—soap is less likely to run into his eyes if the area around them is dry. As

The Expert Knows

Your Schnauzer's Dewclaws

The dewclaws are vestigial toes located partway up a dog's leg from the foot and are so named because they are said to touch the dew on the top of tall grasses (or in a Schnauzer's case, the short grasses). Dewclaws don't touch the ground and serve no purpose.

Chances are that your Schnauzer has come to you with his dewclaws already removed. This is usually done for safety reasons because they can get caught while the dog is hunting or playing. Removal of the dewclaw involves the removal of both the nail and toe, but it's not a complicated procedure and most veterinarians will do it for you if necessary. Unlike docking a dog's tail or cropping his ears, it's not considered a cosmetic procedure.

an extra precaution, you can put a drop of mineral oil into each eye before you bathe him to make sure that the soap isn't going to irritate them. You should also avoid getting water in your dog's ears; not only is it uncomfortable, but moist ears can get infected.

Lather your dog by rubbing your hands against his coat in circles. If you're using a flea shampoo, you may have to let it sit for a few minutes after applying, so stay with your dog, pet and praise him, and don't let him get cold. To prevent your Schnauzer from shaking water and shampoo all over you, hold his ear at the base and

43

he won't be able to shake. When you're done shampooing your dog, rinse out all of the soap thoroughly before you take him out of the bath and dry him with a towel.

How to Bathe Your Schnauzer Outdoors

On a hot summer day, it may be easier to wash your Schnauzer outside in a plastic baby pool or storage bin. Make sure that the water from the hose isn't freezing cold because that's going to be uncomfortable for your dog. Hold him on a leash so that he doesn't run away with his coat full of soap.

Most Schnauzers will dry off on their own while playing outside on a warm day, but make sure that your dog doesn't roll in the dirt after a bath. If the weather is cool or cold, bathe him inside and towel him dry, then blow-dry him on a low or cool setting, brushing gently as you dry to prevent mats. I let my Minis air-dry, and I find that they dry pretty quickly—especially when they rub themselves all over the couch!

Dental Care

Brushing your dog's teeth may seem strange, but it's actually part of routine grooming and is as important as brushing your own teeth. Fortunately, a dog's teeth are not as susceptible to cavities as ours, so they only require cleaning once or twice a week to prevent plaque buildup and encourage gum health.

Brush your Mini's teeth once or twice a week to prevent buildup of plaque.

Once plaque adheres to teeth and becomes tartar, only a thorough cleaning by a veterinarian can remove it. This is an expensive process that usually requires that the dog be put under anesthesia. It's much easier and safer to clean your Schnauzer's teeth routinely at home.

How to Clean Your Dog's Teeth

Use a small piece of gauze, a thin washcloth, or a doggy toothbrush (a little rubber toothbrush that slides over your pointer finger) to clean your dog's teeth. You can also buy special doggy toothpaste that tastes like liver, peanut butter, or chicken. Never use human toothpaste on your dog's teeth because it gets frothy and is far less palatable to a dog. Also, your Schnauzer can't rinse and spit, and toothpaste made for humans should not be swallowed.

Put a small dab of the doggy toothpaste on the toothbrush or gauze, and rub it over the front of your Schnauzer's teeth. Unlike humans, the sides of the teeth that face into a dog's mouth do not require much brushing, if any. The regular movement of the tongue against the teeth is enough to keep them clean on that side.

Dry dog food and crunchy treats scrape away plaque, too, as do hard plastic toys and bones. These simple things, along with regular brushing, can help your Schnauzer avoid stressful, expensive visits to the veterinarian for teeth cleanings.

Ear Care

Canine ears are susceptible to mites and infection, so check them once a month to make sure that they are clean and healthy. You should clean the inside of your Schanuzer's ears as needed (when you notice them becoming a little gunky), or you can clean them routinely after a bath.

SENIOR DOG TIP

Grooming the Older Dog

An older Mini may develop sore muscles or joints and might not want as much intense contact as he once did—both while being groomed and in his daily life. When grooming your older dog, try to avoid any achy or painful spots. When trimming his nails, move his legs slowly and gently. Also, brush him more gently than you would have when he was younger, and always keep him warm during a bath.

If you haven't done so already, get into a teeth-brushing routine with your older dog, and have a veterinarian examine his mouth on a regular basis—plaque on the teeth can affect the gums and lead to infections in the mouth and elsewhere in the body. A thorough teeth cleaning requires anesthesia, which cannot be given to elderly animals or to those with certain health issues.

How to Clean Your Dog's Ears

Your veterinarian or groomer will clean your dog's ears at each visit, but you may want to clean them more often yourself.

To clean your Schnauzer's ears, wrap a warm, soft, damp cloth over your pointer finger and gently wipe down the inside flap of the ear. After that, moisten a cotton ball with ear cleanser, which you can purchase at a pet shop. Do not stick anything deeply into the ear, and only clean the area visible to the eye. It's easy to injure the inside of the ear, so don't use cotton swabs.

The inside of your dog's ears should be the same color as his skin. Red, irritated blotches or other discoloration can indicate a possible ear infection or other problem. Ear infections require a veterinarian's care; do not try to treat them on your own.

Eye Care

Caring for your dog's eyes will help avoid infection and make his face look much cleaner. Do this as often as necessary, but if it seems that your Schnauzer constantly has discharge in his eyes, he might have a health problem that requires veterinary attention.

How to Clean Your Dog's Eyes

To clean your dog's eyes, remove discharge in the corners by wiping them with a moist cloth. If you notice that your dog's brows or eyelashes are obstructing his eyes, trim those hairs carefully.

Nail Care

Long nails can affect a dog's gait and cause foot and leg issues, which will make your Schnauzer very uncomfortable. Often, dogs who regularly walk on pavement or concrete will file their nails down just by walking, but when you hear your dog's nails clacking on hard floors, it's time to have them trimmed. Most dogs don't like having their nails cut, but if they are socialized early to the process, it won't be a big deal.

Clean discharge from your dog's eyes with a moistened cloth.

Trim your dog's nails carefully to avoid cutting the quick.

How to Trim Your Dog's Nails

Your veterinarian or local grooming salon can trim your dog's nails for you, but if you want to do it yourself, you'll need a medium-sized guillotine-style nail clipper that you can purchase at any pet shop. Don't try to use regular scissors or nail clippers intended for humans because they can slip and injure the dog.

Nails contain a blood supply called the "quick" and a dead area above it. You only want to cut the dead area, not the living area that can bleed, as cutting this is very painful for your dog. It's difficult to see the quick of a dark-colored nail, so make conservative cuts and follow up by filing the nail down a little more.

If you accidentally cut the quick, dip the nail into styptic powder (available at your local pet store) or into some flour or cornstarch to stop the bleeding. If you cut the nails every few weeks, the quick will recede and the nails will remain shorter.

Chapter 5

Feeling Good

Keeping your Mini well fed and well groomed is fairly easy, but it's also your job to keep him healthy. This chapter will help you choose the right vet for your dog, and it will also explore some common Schnauzer ailments so that you are better able to recognize potential signs of illness should they appear.

Finding a Veterinarian

There's no question that you need to find an experienced veterinarian with a good bedside manner who clearly loves treating dogs and will explain everything to you thoroughly and patiently. Ideally, you will use the same doctor throughout your dog's life, so it's a relationship that you have to enter into with someone you like who listens to your concerns, answers your questions, and respects both you and your dog. If you establish a good relationship with a veterinarian, you are bound to get much better care if your dog has an emergency, as the doctor will know the dog personally and will have records on any prior health issues.

Do Your Research

You can certainly find a veterinarian in the phone book or see a sign for one in your neighborhood as you're driving by. But rather than use convenience as your guide, you may be better off doing a little research. Ask other dog owners in your neighborhood which veterinarian they use, and see if they're happy with her. Ask about her bedside manner and how good she is at diagnosing conditions. Groomers, dog sitters, and people who work at animal shelters may also be able to guide you in the right direction.

Consider Proximity and Cost

Ideally, your veterinarian's office should be as close as possible to your home—perhaps a ten-minute walk or drive. If there's ever an emergency, you're

Your vet will be one of the most important people in your Mini's life.

going to be happy that your vet is close by. However, if there's a great doctor practicing a little bit farther away, don't count her out. You're better off with someone you and your dog love rather than someone nearby who's not as good or compassionate.

After proximity, consider the cost of the veterinarian. Sure, you don't want to break the bank every time you take your Schnauzer to the vet, but if you hear someone say "That vet is pricey, but she's worth it," take the "she's worth it" part of the recommendation to heart.

Still, even a great vet shouldn't leave you bankrupt. When you call the veterinarian's office, ask how much an

Preparing Your Child for the Dog's Vet Visit

Not many people like taking a trip to the veterinarian—especially children, who might become upset when their puppy has to see the vet. Explain to your child that the doctor is not going to hurt the dog unnecessarily, and even though some of the procedures might be uncomfortable, the puppy is definitely going to get a treat and some nice playtime afterward to help him forget about getting those vaccinations. (You might want to offer to take the child out for some ice cream too!)

To prepare your child for the vet visit, tell her everything she may expect: The pup may be taken in back, where the child can't go. There may be strange noises, like cats mewing loudly or dogs barking. Also, there will be other dogs and cats in the office, and the child should keep her hands to herself—the other animals might be ill and contagious or may not be friendly toward children.

office visit is, how much it charges for annual vaccinations, and how much a "walk-in" fee would be. Also, remember

that your local Humane Society or state-run shelter may offer low-cost vaccinations and even perform spaying and neutering procedures.

Plan an Impromptu Visit

Once you find one or two veterinarians you'd like to consider, pop into the office unexpectedly, without your dog. Ask to take a short tour, if possible, and see where convalescing dogs are kept, as well as the dogs who are boarded overnight. The office should smell clean and look orderly.

Questions to Ask While Visiting

- **Are dogs and cats separated?** It's preferable to have them kept apart from one another in a vet's office.

- **What are the facility's hours?** Find out if it takes emergency calls 24 hours a day. Also, ask if someone stays with the dogs who must stay overnight for surgery.

- **Does it have a specialty?** Some hospitals may specialize in cardiology, orthopedics, oncology, or animal behavior.

- **Does the hospital perform all surgeries and procedures in-house, or are some referred to outside sources?** This is important to know for future reference, in case your dog ever requires a treatment that the hospital can't provide.

- **How many veterinarians work at the facility, and will you be able to choose the one you want?** Will your dog see the same vet each time?

51

Feeling Good

After your dog's initial vet visit, he should return once a year for a regular checkup.

• **Are the employees at the front desk friendly? Are the vet techs helpful, knowledgeable, and amiable?** Vet techs are the people who provide the most hands-on care for the animals who are recovering from surgery or staying overnight, and they often perform small procedures and tests, too. If you get a bad feeling from the vet or the vet techs, do a little more exploring—this isn't the place for you.

Make an Appointment for an Initial Consultation

Once you decide on a veterinary office, make an initial appointment so that you can observe the way the doctor interacts with your dog. She should ask you how old the dog is, how long you have had him, where you got him, and some other basic questions about his history. If your dog isn't neutered or

spayed, the vet probably will discuss this with you.

You will notice the vet checking your Schnauzer's ears, eyes, teeth, gums, skin, and if he's still a puppy, his belly button. She will also palpate your dog's abdomen and check his joints and genitals for abnormalities.

During this initial visit, observe the vet's bedside manner: Is she compassionate? Does she talk a little bit about Schnauzers and their particular medical issues? What's your general feeling about the office? Does your dog get a cookie on the way out?

At this time, you don't have to agree to any medical care—if you just want the checkup, that's fine. You can explain that you're there just to see how the doctor gets along with your dog and make another appointment for medical care at a later date, should you choose.

Find an Emergency Clinic

Even if you just choose a nearby veterinarian out of the phone book, you must find out where the nearest emergency clinic is and how long it takes to get there in case of an emergency. Once you've found a clinic, take a practice run there using the quickest route and look for any possible shortcuts, especially if you live in an area that gets congested with traffic.

The Annual Vet Visit

In the best-case scenario, the only time you and your dog will visit the vet is during your annual visit. Every dog needs a yearly physical, which should include vaccinations and a general checkup to detect parasites, tumors, or other health concerns. This allows your veterinarian to keep on top of your dog's health, weight, coat condition, and overall fitness. She may also ask you to provide a sample of your dog's stool to analyze for worms.

Spaying or Neutering Your Schnauzer

Most people choose to have their Schnauzer spayed (if female) or neutered (if male). Take your veterinarian's recommendations in terms of altering your dog, which usually happens when the dog is six months to one year old. Spaying involves removing all of the sex organs, a more complicated procedure than neutering, which involves castration (removal of the testicles). Both procedures require anesthesia, but a male's recovery time is usually a little quicker than a female's.

The Benefits of Spaying and Neutering

Neutered male dogs tend to be less aggressive and territorial, and the procedure also decreases the dog's desire to roam in search of a female and get into fights. Neutering also decreases a dog's risk for prostate cancer.

Most people spay or neuter their dogs between the ages of six months and one year.

Pet Insurance

Pet insurance works just like health insurance does for humans. It helps cover the cost of expensive health care, including accidents and illnesses, routine preventive care, and often dental cleaning as well. (There are deductibles, just like with human policies.) If you decide to get pet insurance for your Schnauzer, compare various policies before you choose one—and always read the fine print.

Unspayed females go through estrus twice a year for a couple of weeks, which can be an inconvenience for owners. During this time, her scent will attract male dogs from far and wide.

The best reason for altering your dog, however, is to prevent the birth of unwanted puppies. The animal shelters are full of dogs born in homes where the owner "just wanted one litter." The average person isn't equipped to handle dog breeding and the raising of puppies—it's actually a lot more difficult than it may seem and is best left to professional breeders.

Vaccinations

Your veterinarian will recommend a specific vaccination protocol for your puppy. Vaccines are usually first administered when your dog is about six weeks of age and are then given regularly throughout his life, usually once a year. A physical exam always precedes the vaccinations. Puppies should be done weaning and completely healthy before receiving their first vaccines.

Your Mini may receive vaccines against the following diseases, depending on where you live and your vet's recommendations.

- **Bordetella ("kennel cough"):** Bordetella is spread through contact with infected dogs and is generally

Vaccinations protect your dog against a variety of serious illnesses.

not fatal. Symptoms include a raspy, persistent cough.

- **Canine coronavirus:** This is a viral infection that affects the intestinal tract, and a dog can contract it by eating the feces of an infected dog. Symptoms include depression, vomiting, and diarrhea.

- **Distemper:** Distemper is a disease that causes vomiting, diarrhea, pneumonia, and neurological problems. It is an airborne virus easily spread by infected dogs, and it can be fatal.

- **Hepatitis:** Hepatitis is a viral disease that affects the lungs, liver, kidneys, and spleen.

- **Leptospirosis:** This disease affects the liver and kidneys and can be spread to humans through a dog's urine.

- **Lyme disease:** Lyme disease is spread through tick bites and can cause lameness, fever, and joint and muscle damage. Dogs who spend a great deal of time in the woods or outdoors are more likely to contract Lyme disease.

- **Parainfluenza:** Parainfluenza is an infection of the upper respiratory system. Like human influenza, it is very contagious.

- **Rabies:** The rabies vaccine is required by law and is one of the most important vaccinations your dog can receive. Rabies is a viral infection that attacks the nervous system, causing irrational behavior, foaming at the mouth, and

eventually death. It is passed from mammal to mammal—including humans—through a bite from an infected animal.

Don't think that you can shelter your dog from these illnesses. If he walks on a sidewalk, travels to a groomer or veterinarian's office, or goes to the dog park, he is susceptible to them.

Breed-Specific Illnesses

Even with yearly care and the proper preventives, your Schnauzer might still experience medical problems. The following are some illnesses and conditions common in Mini Schnauzers.

Vaccination Side Effects

Most dogs are fine after being vaccinated and exhibit no side effects (although your dog might be sluggish or sore for a few days afterward), but extreme reactions such as hives or vomiting sometimes occur. Tumors can also develop in very rare cases. If you observe any of these reactions in your dog after a vaccination, call your veterinarian immediately.

Making a Doggy First-Aid Kit

Dogs are susceptible to many of the same traumas and ailments that affect humans, such as heat exhaustion, cuts, and allergies, among others. If you purchase or create a doggy first-aid kit and keep it in your home, you can easily begin treatment for small traumas before getting the dog to the veterinarian. Your doggy first-aid kit should include the following:

- antibacterial ointment
- antihistamines
- canine anti-inflammatory
- cloth tape
- eye wash
- gauze bandages
- gauze sponges
- hydrocortisone cream
- hydrogen peroxide
- Pepto-Bismol
- petroleum jelly
- scissors
- self-adhering bandages
- splints

Have your dog's paperwork, regular medicines, a blanket, a thermometer, and a muzzle (in case your dog needs to be restrained) in the kit as well. Take the kit with you on trips, and keep it in an accessible area while at home.

Eye Problems

Mini Schnauzers are prone to a number of eye problems, including congenital cataracts, progressive retinal atrophy, and sudden aquired retinal dystrophy.

Congenital Cataracts

Congenital cataracts are a common problem in Minis. A cataract makes the eye look milky and bluish rather than brown and obstructs the vision, sometimes leaving the dog completely blind.

A veterinarian can examine the eyes of a puppy and see whether cataracts will appear later—usually by the time the dog is one to three years of age. Surgery can correct this condition, but it's difficult and risky. Most dogs with cataracts live just fine being blind—they adapt and overcome.

PRA and SARD

Schnauzers are prone to progressive retinal atrophy (PRA) and sudden acquired retinal dystrophy (SARD). Both involve the death of light receptors in the retina, causing reduced vision, blind spots, and blindness. Sometimes the light receptors are destroyed, and sometimes the retina folds. In extreme cases, a dog might experience retinal separation, cataracts, or enlarged eyes.

Puppies who have PRA generally exhibit symptoms shortly after birth, and a veterinarian should be able to easily detect that something is wrong. Symptoms include slow, progressive blindness. There is no treatment for the condition as of this writing, but

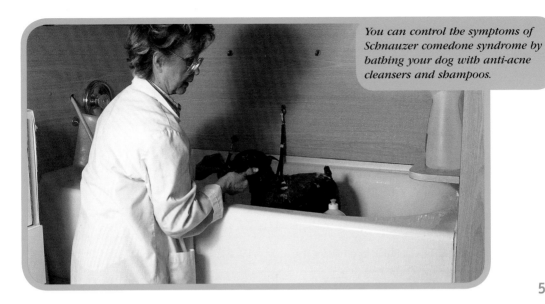

You can control the symptoms of Schnauzer comedone syndrome by bathing your dog with anti-acne cleansers and shampoos.

retinal transplants may be possible in the future.

SARD also causes blindness but does so much more rapidly than PRA—as quickly as a matter of weeks—and the condition doesn't seem to be genetic but is believed to come from autoimmune disease or perhaps toxins in the system. Minis who are more than six years of age can develop SARD, and there is no treatment as of this writing.

Hypothyroidism
Hypothyroidism is a decrease in thyroid hormone that tends to affect dogs between the ages of two and six years. Symptoms occur gradually and can include listlessness, lethargy, depression, weight gain, personality change, hair loss, cold intolerance, and drowsiness. Symptoms may also include thickening or darkening of the skin, a decreased heart rate, and seizures or stumbling. Hypothyroidism can be treated by administering a synthetic thyroid hormone for the duration of the afflicted dog's life.

Schnauzer Comedone Syndrome
Schnauzers often suffer from a skin condition called Schnauzer comedone syndrome, a type of seborrhea (excessive discharge from the sebaceous glands). Symptoms include skin scaling and blackheads (keratin plugs blocking the hair follicles), but the condition usually doesn't bother the dog unless the blemishes become infected. The syndrome is incurable, but it is controllable with the use of anti-acne cleansing products and antiseborrheic shampoos.

Parasites
Parasites live on or inside your dog and can create health problems ranging in

severity from minor and irritating to potentially life threatening. Here are a few of the most common parasites that can plague a Schnauzer.

Use a safe insecticide to protect your dog from fleas both indoors and outdoors.

External Parasites

External parasites feed on a dog's blood, causing him irritation and skin problems.

Fleas

If you've ever had a dog or cat, you are probably familiar with fleas, the most common parasite affecting dogs. Fleabites cause itching and can create severe allergic reactions or even a tapeworm infestation in some cases. Fleas bite humans as well and can eventually infest an entire house. Once they entrench themselves in a home, they become even more difficult to eliminate.

Your first defense in the battle against fleas is prevention. Have your veterinarian sell you a topical application to spread between your Schnauzer's shoulder blades. This pesticide controls fleas and their eggs without harming your dog. There are similar over-the-counter products that will kill fleas or eggs, but not both. Once you're done preventing fleas on your dog, use a safe insecticide in your home and in outdoor areas, especially in the warm summer months. Your vet can also give your dog pills that will sterilize any flea that bites him, which will eventually lead to total extermination as long as the

fleas in your home don't find someone else to bite.

To combat an already existing flea infestation on your dog, use a flea shampoo or a dip (which you pour over the dog) if it's a really bad case. Your veterinarian can help you determine the best products to use on your dog. You can also have your local groomer give him a flea treatment.

Mites

There are two types of mites typically found on dogs: sarcoptic and demodex mites. Both of these mites cause a skin condition called mange, the symptoms of which include intense itching, hair loss, crusty bumps on the skin (which may have a rotting odor), and lesions at the edges of the ears.

Sarcoptic mites, or scabies, are highly contagious among dogs and can infest humans as well. This type of mange is tough to diagnose and may be mistaken for other skin conditions as it worsens. If you suspect that your dog has scabies, rub the inner edge of his ear with your finger and see if he pedals his leg on the same side in a scratching motion (similar to the kicking he does when you scratch his belly in a spot he likes). If he does this, he probably has sarcoptic mites and will need treatment, which will include several insecticidal dips (performed by your vet) and perhaps an injection of Ivermectin, an antiparasite medication administered by a vet.

The demodex mite causes symptoms similar to those caused by the sarcoptic mite, but they are less intense. This mite can also infest humans, although this rarely happens. Veterinarians diagnose demodex mites by examining a skin scraping under a microscope, and they treat the infestation with several insecticidal dips. (This is the kind of mange that my Mini, Pepper, had when I first got him from the shelter. It took six months to eliminate with insecticidal dips, and the treatment was quite rough on him.)

Ringworm

Ringworm isn't actually a worm—it's a fungus that grows on the skin and

SENIOR DOG TIP

Keeping Your Senior Schnauzer Healthy

Schnauzers are considered senior citizens when they are about ten years old or so, although the aging process varies from dog to dog. Aging Schnauzers may start to show some signs of slowing down, including hearing loss, change in coat, joint stiffness, arthritis, and a decreased ability to fight off disease. Ask your veterinarian about a senior diet, and make sure to keep up with health exams. Also, remember that your older Schnauzer isn't as spry as he once was, and he may need help getting in and out of the car or his bed.

causes patches of hair loss and itching. It is also transmittable to humans. Your veterinarian can diagnose ringworm visually, but a culture of the affected area can also help diagnose the fungus. Treatment includes fungicidal shampoos, creams, and in some cases, oral medication.

Ticks

Ticks are another pesky external parasite, especially for dogs who like to play outside. Ticks can spread disease through their bites—most notably Lyme disease but also Rocky Mountain spotted fever, babesiosis, and ehrlichiosis. Their presence on your dog's skin isn't as obvious as with fleas; you will discover ticks only by thoroughly examining your dog, including near his eyes, tail, and inside the ears. The tick will feel like a small bump on the skin. Often, people discover ticks while they are petting or brushing their dog.

To remove a tick, grip it close to the skin with a pair of tweezers and pull it out slowly. Do not jerk or twist the tick out. You want to make sure to get all of the tick, including the mouth parts, which will be hanging on tightly. Infection can occur from leaving the mouth parts in the skin after removing the rest of the tick. If you can't get the tick's head out, take your dog to the veterinarian.

Once you remove the tick, put it in a plastic baggie or container and take it to the veterinarian for testing to make sure that it didn't pass a disease to your dog. Clean your Schnauzer's wound with rubbing alcohol or another disinfectant to minimize the chance of infection.

Internal Parasites

Internal parasites are less easy to see than external parasites, but they are no less of a nuisance. Do not disregard the symptoms of internal parasites—they can be deadly to your dog.

Heartworms

Heartworms are a problem for dogs, especially those who live in a moist, hot climate. Heartworms can live as parasites in various animals, but they prefer dogs. They are transmitted through mosquitoes carrying infected blood. Microfilariae—heartworms in their larval form—enter the dog's body from the mosquito and travel to the heart and arteries, where they grow and reproduce. Heartworms can grow to be 1 foot (0.3 m) long and can live up to seven years.

Afflicted dogs may not exhibit symptoms until up to a year after infestation. Infestation usually begins with a cough, labored breathing, and weight loss, and then eventually leads to kidney and liver damage as the infestation worsens. The dog will seem lethargic and tired and may lose consciousness in later stages of the infestation. The prognosis for a dog at this stage is poor, and he will eventually die if the heartworms aren't treated.

Your veterinarian can use blood tests and X-rays to diagnose the presence of heartworms but not until the mature worms have been inside the dog for at least six to seven months.

Careful Cleaning

When cleaning your dog's ears, never, ever use a cotton swab because you can injure your dog's ear if the swab goes too deeply inside. Only use cotton balls and your finger, and be gentle.

Treatment includes medication and possibly surgery to remove the worms from the heart.

Fortunately, there are monthly heartworm preventives that your veterinarian can provide that can prevent your dog from contracting heartworms. The vet will start your Schnauzer on these treatments once he has tested negative for heartworms.

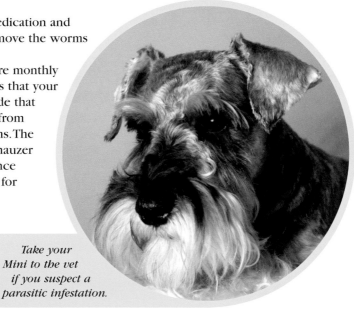

Hookworms

Hookworms are nasty parasites that attach to a dog's intestines and feed on his blood, causing anemia and digestive disorders. A stool sample analyzed by a veterinarian can show the presence of hookworms, which are treatable with one of many common deworming medications. Your dog's monthly heartworm preventive also prevents hookworms.

Take your Mini to the vet if you suspect a parasitic infestation.

Roundworms

Roundworms infest the small intestine and interfere with digestion. They can give the afflicted dog a shabby, malnourished appearance and swollen belly and can cause anemia and even pneumonia as the larvae move through the respiratory system. Roundworms transfer from mother to puppy during gestation or nursing. A dog can also contract roundworms by ingesting roundworm eggs (often by eating another animal infested with the parasite). The worms show up in feces (and vomit), so your veterinarian can test a stool sample to detect them in your dog.

Treatment with a common dewormer is effective against mature roundworms but has to be repeated after two weeks to kill the larvae that matured after the initial treatment.

Whipworms

Whipworms infest a dog's large intestine and cecum (appendix), causing digestive disorders such as recurring diarrhea. Eventually, the damage these worms do may cause a bacterial infection to thrive. A dog gets whipworms by eating infected soil, so dogs who walk in or eat soil and then lick their feet are at risk. Treatment with a common dewormer is effective. Your

Feeling Good

dog's heartworm preventive will also work on whipworms.

General Illnesses

The following are some diseases and ailments that can affect all types of dogs, regardless of breed.

Allergies

Food allergies in dogs are common, as are allergies to fleas, dust mites, and mold. The main symptom of allergies is itchiness, which results in hair loss and open sores due to frequent scratching. An afflicted dog may also lick and chew on his legs and paws. If you suspect that your dog has allergies, take him to the veterinarian because itching can be the result of a number of other illnesses as well.

Food allergies are usually diagnosed by eliminating one individual element at a time from the dog's diet and replacing it with something he hasn't had before until the symptoms go away. Then you can add the eliminated food items back into the diet one at a time to see if the dog has an allergic reaction. Once the reaction returns, you'll know which

ingredient is causing the allergy. Your veterinarian can also test your dog's skin to try to determine the cause of the allergy.

Medications such as topical ointments, steroid shots, and antihistamines can make your dog more comfortable when he's exhibiting symptoms.

Cancer

Dogs can get cancer in any of their organs, and the symptoms a dog exhibits will vary depending on the type of cancer and where it occurs. Take your dog to the veterinarian if you

Dogs are prone to many of the same allergies that can affect humans.

Your dog may benefit from treatment with a combination of complementary and traditional medicine.

notice a growth or tumor anywhere on your dog, if he is wheezing or coughing, or if he has unexplained weight loss.

Cancer in dogs is treated similarly to cancer in humans, and some forms of the disease are easier to treat than others. To help prevent cancer in your dog, spay your female before her first heat cycle, which will protect her from cancers of the reproductive organs. Neuter your male dog, especially if his testes haven't descended. Also, keep your dog away from carcinogens, such as cigarette smoke, and limit his exposure to pesticides (including flea and tick preventives).

Cushing's Disease
Older dogs sometimes develop hyperadrenocorticism, also called Cushing's disease. This disease is characterized by a tumor either on the pituitary gland (in 85 percent of cases) or on the adrenal gland (in 15 percent of cases) that causes the affected gland to produce too much adrenocorticotrophic hormone (in the case of the pituitary gland) or too much cortisol (in the case of the adrenal gland). This puts the body's natural chemistry out of balance and brings on symptoms including an increase in appetite, panting, high blood pressure, changes in skin color and texture, hair loss, thirstiness, more frequent urination, a bulging abdomen, and nervous system disorders.

These symptoms are sometimes mistaken for other health issues, but Cushing's disease can be fatal if left untreated—an afflicted dog may succumb to heart failure, liver failure, or infection. Treatment includes medications and surgery and can begin once a diagnosis is made through a blood test.

Diabetes

Dogs can also get diabetes, especially (but not exclusively) overweight dogs. Diabetes is the result of a hormone imbalance, which causes symptoms including excessive drinking, frequent urination, and weight loss. If a dog's diabetes is left untreated, he can eventually develop serious health issues such as kidney problems and cataracts.

Dogs with diabetes require insulin injections to regulate their blood sugar. Some diabetic dogs can also benefit from the use of a specialized diet and exercise program.

Ear Infections

Buildup of moisture or wax in the ear canal can cause ear infections, as can the presence of mites in the ear. Infected ears have a sweet, rotten smell and may also have a sticky brown or yellow substance inside them. A dog will scratch his ears and shake his head frequently to relieve irritation, so take him to the veterinarian if you witness this behavior and suspect an ear infection.

Treatment usually consists of cleaning out the ear every day with a special solution, a course of antibiotics, and keeping the ear free of hair and moisture. Some over-the-counter remedies can also work well to prevent or clear up ear infections.

Eye Infections

Eye infections can happen as the result of an injury, a foreign body or chemicals getting into the eye, dental problems, dehydration, or any disease that causes the eye to dry out. Symptoms include red eyelids, watery eyes, and frequent scratching of the eyes. If you suspect a foreign substance or an injury, flush the eye with saline solution and see if that relieves the symptoms. If it doesn't, take your dog to the veterinarian as soon as possible.

Alternative Therapies

Today, many veterinarians are trained in alternative therapies (also known as complementary medicine) that can be used in conjunction with traditional medical practices.

Alternative therapies should only be administered by licensed professionals. Herbs and supplements might not seem dangerous, but they can be very powerful and may cause unwelcome side effects.

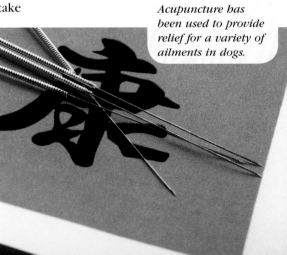

Acupuncture has been used to provide relief for a variety of ailments in dogs.

Even though an alternative therapy should not be the main source of medical treatment, it might help an ill dog feel more comfortable. In particular, allergies and arthritis are often treated somewhat successfully using alternative treatments. Vitamins, chondroitin sulfate, glucosamine, and fatty acid supplements have all been reported to offer some relief to dogs with degenerative joint diseases.

Acupuncture

Acupuncture is an ancient method of healing that involves sticking very fine needles into specific points in the body to get the body's natural energy flowing. Dogs can react very well to this treatment and find relief for a variety of ailments, from arthritis and lameness to sinusitis and circulatory problems and many more. It's worth asking your veterinarian about a licensed veterinary acupuncturist in your area if your dog has a chronic disorder or is experiencing acute pain.

Herbal Therapy

Many herbs have proven useful for aiding the treatment of a variety of illnesses. Herbal therapy is part of a holistic treatment that works to help the body heal itself by boosting the immune system. As with homeopathic treatments, there are countless herbal

The Expert Knows

What Is a Holistic Veterinarian?

A holistic veterinarian evaluates an animal's health by taking into account the whole body and how it works as a system, including emotional factors like stress and the animal's relationship with his owner. Holistic medicine includes treatments that center around herbal medicine, dietary needs, homeopathy, chiropractic, behavior modification, augmentation therapy, and acupuncture, in conjunction with traditional medicine. You can find a holistic veterinarian the same way you would find a traditional veterinarian—by word of mouth or by recommendation—or you can contact the American Holistic Veterinary Medical Association (AHVMA) at www.ahvma.org.

therapies that help with various symptoms and diseases.

Homeopathy

Homeopathy is a practice that was founded in the early 1800s. Its creator believed that the body could heal itself when stimulated by substances that create the same type of symptoms that a patient's illness is causing. This belief is called the Law of Similars. There are books on alternative treatments for dogs that detail what kinds of substances can address specific symptoms.

Chapter 6

Being Good

Training your dog is absolutely necessary, especially for a high-energy, spirited, self-directed dog like the Miniature Schnauzer. Dogs don't train themselves to be well-behaved members of the household. They will behave however they desire to get what they need. In the case of a Schnauzer, that may mean barking, jumping on guests for attention, and not following commands (especially if there's something fun to chase instead!). Fortunately, you can manage all of these undesired behaviors and many others with just a little training.

Training your dog is no inconsequential task, but it's also easier than you may think. You just have to get into your dog's head and see the world as he sees it. He's a simple being, and he is programmed to do what works for him. Proper training just shows your dog clearly and simply what you want him to do and what you don't want him to do.

Positive Training

Positive training, in which you reward your dog for desired behaviors (usually with treats, praise, or play) and ignore unwanted behaviors rather than punishing him for them, is the most effective way to get your pet to do what you want him to do. Studies have shown that organisms are more likely to repeat a behavior that is rewarding for them than they are to stop a behavior due to a resulting punishment.

Remember that what you think of as "positive" or "negative" attention might mean something else to your dog. To him, a little eye contact, saying his name, and touching him are all generally positive. When he runs away from you and you chase him yelling his name, that's positive too—he thinks it's a game! When he jumps up on your leg and you push him off, he's just happy that you're touching him.

For positive training to work, you have to completely ignore all unwanted behaviors and only praise desired behaviors. For example, imagine you're in the dog park and your dog isn't coming when called. Rather than chasing him and getting angry, wait until he looks for you—and he *will* look for you eventually—and then praise him for looking at you and show him that you have a treat (which should be enough to make him come running).

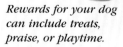

Rewards for your dog can include treats, praise, or playtime.

Keep Sessions Short and Sweet

Training sessions for puppies should happen a few times a day for no more than two to five minutes at a time. (For an adolescent dog, training sessions can last 10 to 15 minutes, while adults can train for about 20 minutes or until the dog gets tired or bored.) Don't make training sessions too long; wrap up before you wear out your dog's attention span. If he gets bored or tired or is consistently unsuccessful during a session, it defeats the purpose of training.

This type of training allows the dog to use his brain and solve problems on his own. If, for example, he always gets his food when he sits nicely as you hold his dish, he will always sit nicely before a meal. If you withhold his food until he sits, he will come to understand what you want of him.

Clicker Training

Clicker training is a popular method these days and for good reason—it uses positive reinforcement and allows a dog to figure out problems on his own. The clicker is a small noisemaker that "marks" a desired behavior. After a click, the dog gets a treat. (If you don't have a clicker, a verbal "Yes!" or similar word can mark a behavior in the same way.) Eventually, he will begin to connect the click with something good and will work to earn a click.

Priming the Clicker

To begin clicker training, you have to first make your dog understand that a click means he has done something right. Start off by "priming" the clicker: Click and then immediately give your dog a small treat. You should prime the clicker a few times before every training session; you want to create an association in your dog's mind between the click and the treat. Once you can click and have him look up attentively, you know that he has associated the click with the treat, and you can move on with the training session.

Shaping Behavior With the Clicker

When you're teaching your dog the basic commands (also called cues), you should only click when he offers the desired behavior. Let's say that you want to teach the *sit* command. Your dog will know that you have a treat in your hand, and he will wonder how to get it. Perhaps he'll jump on you or bark—but those aren't the behaviors you're looking for. Eventually he will sit down, puzzled—and that's when you click and treat him. Wow! He'll wonder what he did to get the treat, and he will try some other behaviors. Then, he will sit again—and you click and treat again. He'll quickly come to realize that when his hind end hits the floor he gets a treat, so he will start offering a *sit* whenever you have treats. Now you can add the verbal cue, "sit," just as he's sitting, and then click and treat. He will come to associate the word "sit" with the behavior.

Let's say that your Schnauzer doesn't offer a *sit*, but his hind end goes down a bit. You can also click on that. Perhaps he'll then put his hind end down even more—click on that. After that, you click only for the correct behavior unless the dog really doesn't seem to be getting it, in which case you can start from step one again. This process, in which you click for small increments of progress toward a desired behavior until it is reached, is called shaping.

Timing and Positivity

There are two critical things to remember when clicker training. The first is that you have to click at just the right moment—when the behavior you want is happening. You should click as your dog's butt is going down or exactly at the moment it reaches the ground. If you click too late, while your dog is getting up from the *sit*, he will not know what you're praising and may think that what you want is for him to get up, not sit down.

The second most important thing to remember is that you have to allow the dog to feel successful in his training. Don't be a stingy trainer; treat generously or you will just frustrate your dog

and yourself. Make him feel as if he's "getting it." If what you're trying to teach him is too difficult for that day, go back to something he does know and let him feel a sense of accomplishment. Always end a training session on a positive note.

Socialization

Socialization is about introducing a puppy to everything he might encounter as an adult dog. An unsocialized dog may view new people, animals, and situations with suspicion or fear.

The puppy socialization period occurs when the puppy is about 4 to 20 weeks old. During this time, he is still soaking in his world, learning about life and everything in it. At this stage,

A well-socialized Mini is comfortable and confident around new people, children, and other animals.

Training Treats

The treats you use when training your dog should be small and moist. Very small bits of hot dog or cheese work well. Some companies make soft morsels specifically for training. At the end of a training session, you can give him a big crunchy bone or stuffed toy, but only after you're done. The treats should also be fragrant (stinky) so that your dog is eager for them—he'll pay more attention to you when he knows that something good is coming his way.

Every now and then—say, every tenth time your Mini performs a good behavior—offer treats "jackpot style," giving him a bunch at a time. This will keep his attention and make him wonder when the next jackpot is coming, the same way a slot machine works.

Some Schnauzers learn well with treats, but others will love a squeaky toy or just lavish praise for especially good behavior. Find out what your dog likes best, and use that as your reward.

a puppy is eager to accept new things with interest, and you should introduce your Schnauzer to as many new people, animals, objects, surfaces, types of touch, and situations as possible. After 20 weeks it becomes a lot harder to socialize a dog because his view of the world has been set, and he's not going to be eager to change.

Socializing Your Puppy to People, Places, and Things

Make every new situation, person, and object fun and pleasant for your puppy. If something scares him before he's 20 weeks old, he might be afraid of it for the rest of his life. For example, if he has a bad time riding in a car when he's a puppy, he may always fear the car or get carsick. The same goes for the grooming salon, vet's office, and so on.

It's important not to let anything traumatize your puppy. While he's still learning about life's situations, keep his world calm and pleasant. Allow strangers to pet him and give him treats. Introduce him to people of all shapes, colors, ages, and sizes, and make every new meeting fun.

Also make sure that he meets different dogs of all sizes and shapes. Only intervene in playtime if it gets too rough; otherwise, let the dogs tumble and play. Allow your Schnauzer to meet other pets such as cats, small animals, and birds, but supervise all interspecies meetings carefully.

Socializing Your Puppy to Children

It is critical that you socialize your dog to children. Even though kids are little,

Children can be intimidating to a dog who hasn't been properly socialized to them.

they can be very intimidating to a dog. It's not really your own children you have to worry about (as long as your children already know the proper way to interact with the dog) but rather kids your Mini doesn't know who might run up to him, tease him, or pull his ears and stubby tail. Kids move fast and erratically, and they can be loud, all of which may scare a puppy.

Socialize your puppy to children at a young age by having him learn to accept touch in places where a child might touch him, like the ears, tail, paws, and muzzle. Introduce your dog to this gradually by touching each of these areas briefly and then offering him a treat. When he's used to being touched, touch each place again for a longer duration before you offer a treat. Next, gently tug the ears and tail, then treat him. Gently hold his muzzle closed for a moment, then treat. If you get your dog used to different ways of being touched, hopefully it won't bother him when a stranger does it.

Finally, enlist some mature neighborhood kids to play with your puppy, but let them know the ground rules: They have to be gentle and kind. Always supervise all interactions between your dog and children.

Crate Training

Putting a puppy into a crate or kennel may seem like punishment or a way to give him a "time-out," but the crate is actually an effective training

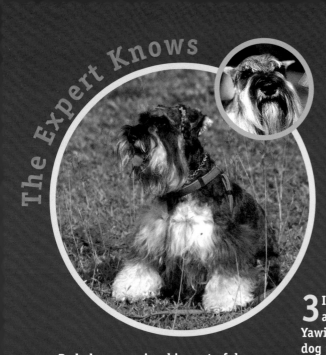

Body Language

Body language is a big part of dog communication, so your Schnauzer will be watching you for clues on how you're feeling and how he should behave. Here are some tips on body language when training your dog:

1 Don't stoop or kneel. This is tough with a smaller dog like the Mini—you're going to have to do some stooping, obviously—but do your best to limit it. Making yourself smaller or putting yourself on the dog's level may show him that you're being submissive.

2 Don't glare at a fearful dog but instead look indirectly at him with your body turned away.

3 If you have a fearful dog, yawn and sigh to put him at ease. Yawing is a calming signal used in dog packs that is believed to diffuse tension. (You might notice your dog yawning during stressful situations.) Yawning in a dog pack may also signal that it's time to settle down for the evening.

4 Dogs often show dominance by mounting. If your dog is mounting you or other family members, put him back on the floor so that he has all four feet touching the ground, then place one hand on his shoulders and one on his back and keep them firmly placed there for a few moments. Don't be forceful—just show him that you're the alpha dog in the house and that you may touch him like this, but not the other way around.

Dogs are den animals who feel safest in small, enclosed spaces.

device, and most dogs come to appreciate having a place where they can go to chill out or have a nap. Choose a spot for your dog's crate, preferably in a corner of a quiet room, but not so out of the way that the dog feels isolated from the family.

Dogs are denning animals, and it's their instinct to like small, dark, safe places. This is why dogs often sleep under tables or in a corner—it makes them feel secure. Most dogs who are crate trained using positive training come to love the crate and will use it as a favorite sleeping place—the crate becomes a dog's den. I leave two crates open and on the floor at all times with a soft bed and chew toy in each, and my Minis use them as napping spots. (See Chapter 2 for help on how to properly choose the right kind of crate for your Mini.)

How to Crate Train Your Dog

Crate training, like obedience training, should be done using positive training. Provide plenty of praise and treats throughout the training process, from when you first introduce your Mini to the crate to when he can be comfortable and quiet in there for hours at a time.

Your dog should never be in a position to use his crate as a potty spot. That defeats the purpose of the crate. He should only stay inside his crate for as long as he can "hold it," perhaps a couple of hours for a puppy, perhaps less; even an adult dog should not spend more than six hours in his crate at once. Gauge your puppy's "holding power" and take him out of his crate to eliminate well before he absolutely needs to go.

Introducing Him to the Crate

If you can, take the door off of the crate and lure your puppy inside with a treat. Once he goes into the crate, click and treat him for being inside. When he comes out, stop petting and praising him, then repeat the first step. The idea is to show him that being in the crate is fun and that you're happy when he goes in by himself.

If your puppy won't go inside the crate without serious prodding, reward him for setting a paw at the edge of or just inside the crate. Try to lure him further, and praise him for each step he takes closer to being inside the crate. Don't just pick him up and shove him inside; let going inside be his idea. (You may want to put some treats at the back of the crate to help things along.) Remember, at some point you're going to lock him in, and if you do it without socializing him to the crate first, he's going to view it as punishment rather than his own private space.

Getting Used to the Crate

Once your puppy gets the hang of walking in and out of the crate by himself, you can put the door back onto it and then repeat the steps again, this time closing the crate for a second while he's inside and then opening it again. Repeat this procedure until you can close the crate for a few moments without him getting upset and crying to be let out. Open the door well before that happens, but do not under any circumstances try to console your puppy if he whines—remember, he gets a treat for wanted behaviors but ignored for unwanted behaviors.

Next, leave your Schnauzer confined inside the crate while you get up and step away. If he's calm, come back, then click and treat him for being calm and

While housetraining, praise your Mini each time he eliminates outdoors.

happy inside the crate, and then let him out. Repeat these steps until you can walk all the way across the room while he remains calm and quiet inside the crate.

One trick is to give your dog something really good to chew while he's in the crate, like a rubber toy stuffed with his favorite food. If he's distracted with a treat, he won't have time to be too upset.

Remember to make every step of training fun. If your Mini is whining, scratching at the crate's door, or becoming upset, just quit the training session for the day—but not before you can get one calm second from him when he's in the crate. Always end each session on a positive note.

If you use this method of crate training, you will gradually work up to being able to leave the room with your dog in his crate, then being able to leave the house, all while your dog is calm and content chewing on a bone or stuffed toy. When you're not using the crate for confinement, leave the door open and make sure that there's a nice fluffy bed or crate pad inside so that he can use the crate as a bed.

Housetraining

Start housetraining your puppy the minute you bring him home. Watch for signs that he needs to eliminate, and anticipate that moment—this is the only way to get him to his designated potty spot in time. Signs of a puppy needing to eliminate include turning around in circles, sniffing a certain area, and squatting—but by the time he's squatting, it's usually too late. Some dogs don't give any indication at all that they need to go, however, so just remember to take your pup out as frequently as possible.

Minis are easily distracted outdoors, but they can still learn to reliably come when called.

Children and Training

Kids are great at helping to teach the *recall* command. Using one or more kids, start a game by putting the children at opposite points of the yard or park (with a long line on the dog—do not let him loose), and give the kids dog treats. Have them take turns calling the dog by name and using the *recall* command ("Fido, come!") and treating him when he responds. Be careful about allowing children to teach any other commands, however, because a few slipups can set training back. Also, if the dog isn't responding or the kids get out of hand while calling him, stop the game for the day.

Usually, puppies need to potty in the morning, just after meals, after waking up from a nap, and before bed. Once you have an idea of your puppy's bathroom schedule, you can pick him up and walk him outdoors to the area where you want him to go.

How to Housetrain Your Dog

When your puppy eliminates in the area where you want him to, praise him and offer him treats. If you catch him in the act of eliminating inside where he shouldn't, say "No!" sharply to get his attention, then pick him up immediately and take him to the spot you'd like him to use. Don't make a big deal about it.

If you notice after the fact that he has eliminated inside, there's nothing you can do to teach him a lesson. Don't punish the dog or rub his nose in it. These tactics offer little instruction and actually teach your Mini that elimination itself is wrong and that he should fear you. Instead, reward your dog when he properly eliminates outside, and he will most likely continue to potty there.

Teaching Basic Commands

All well-behaved dogs should know a few basic behaviors. These behaviors keep dogs safe and make them more pleasant to be around. A well-trained dog is also less likely to be given up to a shelter and lives a much better life than one who's allowed to run amok and do whatever he wants.

Come (Recall)

The most important command, or cue, that you can teach your dog is the *recall*, which you use to get your dog to come to you. Sounds simple, doesn't it? For some dogs, however, it's actually quite difficult. Schanuzers in particular can get very distracted outside, but for the most part they are good at coming when called if you teach the command properly from the beginning. When your dog has mastered the *recall* command, you should be able to say your dog's name, followed by the word "come," to get him to come right to you.

There are only two situations in which you should need to use your dog's name: to call him to you or to get his attention. In both cases, use his name positively. Never use his name to scold him, and never call him to you to reprimand him. After all, what's the point of coming to you if he's just going to get punished?

How to Teach Recall

The first step in teaching the *recall* is getting your dog to pay attention to you. There are many other things that can capture his attention, but you have to be the most interesting. This is why you have treats!

With some treats in one hand, click and say your dog's name. When he looks at you, even for a moment, click and toss a treat his way. Continue this game until he's coming over to you for a treat whenever you call him. If he doesn't look your way, just wait until he does. Don't continue to call his name or get frustrated if he's not responding. Just wait until he looks your way eventually, and then praise and treat him.

Next, put him on a 15- to 25-foot (4.6- to 7.6-m) leash, and take him outside along with your treats and

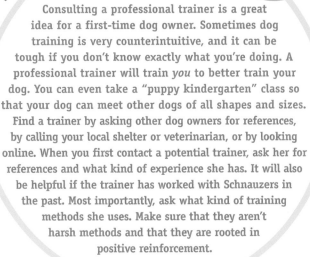

The Expert Knows

Finding a Trainer

Consulting a professional trainer is a great idea for a first-time dog owner. Sometimes dog training is very counterintuitive, and it can be tough if you don't know exactly what you're doing. A professional trainer will train *you* to better train your dog. You can even take a "puppy kindergarten" class so that your dog can meet other dogs of all shapes and sizes. Find a trainer by asking other dog owners for references, by calling your local shelter or veterinarian, or by looking online. When you first contact a potential trainer, ask her for references and what kind of experience she has. It will also be helpful if the trainer has worked with Schnauzers in the past. Most importantly, ask what kind of training methods she uses. Make sure that they aren't harsh methods and that they are rooted in positive reinforcement.

clicker. Let him explore the yard or park to the end of the lead, and then call him to you. If he seems reluctant, encourage him to come by showing him a treat. Click as he runs toward you, and treat when he reaches you. If you click as he's coming toward you, he will associate the act of coming to you with the treat. If you click when he reaches you, he may associate the click with jumping on you or taking the treat.

If you can get someone else to help teach the *recall* command, sit or stand a few feet (meters) apart and make a game of calling your dog to and from each person, moving farther apart as the dog becomes more successful at the game. Once it's clear that he understands what he's supposed to do, add the word "come" to his name. Always say his name and the command in a very excited and fun tone, and encourage him to come to you by patting your leg and clucking your tongue.

Sit

The *sit* command is not only important for a well-behaved dog but can also save his life in an emergency. Imagine that he gets off his leash accidentally, rushes out the door, and runs toward the street—and oncoming traffic. If you have consistently reinforced the *sit* command, you can yell "Sit!" and there's a good chance he'll obey.

How to Teach Sit

Stand in front of your dog with him on his leash facing you. Hold a fragrant treat between your thumb and index finger right over his nose, then move your hand slowly back toward his tail. His head should follow the treat, and his rear should move downward into a *sit*. When this happens, click and give him the treat. If he won't sit, begin shaping the behavior by clicking for approximations of a *sit*: first for his rear lowering a little, then for lowering a little more, and eventually for a full *sit*. (Be sure not to skimp on treats!)

Sometimes a dog will spin around to get at the treat rather than move his head back and put his behind down, or sometimes he will jump up to get it. If he does this, try again, but shaping might not be the best way to teach this individual dog to sit. You might have to use the modeling technique, which requires you to gently guide the dog into a sitting position while telling him to sit.

Sit is one of the easiest commands to teach your dog.

Once he has gotten the hang of sitting for a treat, let your Mini think for a moment before luring him into another *sit*. He most likely will offer you a *sit* on his own to see if that's what's getting him all those yummy treats. When he sits on his own, click and treat again. Now he'll understand what you want and start sitting like crazy to get those treats. Add a verbal cue, and he'll come to associate the word "sit" with the behavior. But don't add the cue too soon, or you'll confuse him—wait until your dog seems to really understand what you're looking for.

If your dog is slow to respond to the verbal cue, don't get frustrated and repeat "Sit! Sit! Sit!" over and over again. Your dog heard you the first time—he's not deaf. Just wait for him to offer you the behavior. If you have treats in your hand while using the clicker, he will definitely try to figure out what you want without you having to repeat yourself.

Down

Down is an important command. You may want your dog to lie down when you need him out of the way or when a wary stranger approaches. It's also good for getting your dog to settle down when he's hyped up.

Teaching the *down* command is a little more difficult than teaching *sit* because lying down is a submissive position, and some dogs don't like it. However, Mini Schnauzers do aim to please, so if you have the right

Use a treat to lure your Mini into the down position.

You can teach your dog to stay in either a sit or down position.

motivation (a pocket full of liver snacks and some really hardy praise) you can teach them just about anything.

How to Teach Down

Starting with your dog in the *sit* position, place a treat inside your hand and let him smell it so that he knows it's there. Next, move your hand downward toward the floor, and slide it along the floor away from his nose. If he gets up to get the treat, put him back into the *sit* and try again. Ideally, your dog should wiggle into a semi-*down* or a full *down* position as he's following the treat with his nose. Once his elbows touch the floor, click and treat. Repeat and add the verbal cue "down" once he begins to offer the behavior on his own.

You may have to shape this behavior by clicking and treating for small increments toward the *down* position. For example, once your dog gets good at bowing down, raise the criteria for which you click and treat to when his elbows reach the floor, then his chest, and so on until he's in a complete *down*. Remember to click as he's getting into position, not as he's getting up, or he'll learn the wrong behavior. Once he learns how to go into the *down* from the *sit* and understands the "down" cue, try getting him to go into a *down* from a standing position using the same method.

Stay

Stay is difficult to teach because it requires that your dog do nothing, whereas most trained behaviors require action on his part. It's an especially tough command for a Mini, an easily distracted dog who might take off on a whim after a paper bag blowing down the street. Don't get your hopes up for a 20-minute *stay* in a park full of kids, squirrels, and other dogs, but with time and dedication, you should be able to teach your Mini a long enough *stay* to save his life in an emergency situation or for when you just need to turn your back on him for a moment.

How to Teach Stay

Put your Mini into a *sit* or *down*, and then stand in front of him. Hold your flattened palm a couple of feet (meters) from his face and say "Stay" in a firm tone. Wait a second, then click and treat him while he's still sitting. He will probably get up at this point, which is fine as long as you clicked and treated

while he was sitting or down. Gradually work up to more time in the *stay,* and then vary the time you require your dog to stay in each lesson. For example, ask for 3 seconds, then 20 seconds, then 2 seconds, then 1 minute, and so on.

The release is an important part of the *stay* command. You don't want your dog to just get up out of the *stay* whenever he wants; that defeats the purpose of the command. Choose a release word, like "okay," and say it when you want your dog to come out of the *stay*. Once he understands that "okay" means he can get up, only click and treat him upon saying "okay" when you're reinforcing the *stay* command.

Always treat while your dog is in the *stay*, or he'll think that the behavior you are rewarding is the release. This isn't easy, and you may have setbacks, but that's okay. Just go back to step one if your dog breaks a *stay*.

Walking Nicely on a Leash

Although a Schnauzer isn't a big dog, it's no fun walking any dog if he's trying to drag you down the block. The Mini is small but persistent, and he will want to get where he wants to go in a hurry.

Clicker Training the Older Dog

Don't think that old dogs can learn new tricks? That myth is as outdated as 8-tracks. Clicker training is great for teaching older dogs new commands or tricks. Old dogs may know some commands already, but they may not know them well. Use the clicker to hone and sharpen the commands your dog has already learned.

For example, you may want a nice, square sit instead of a sloppy plop-down; or your older dog might come out of a stay whenever he wants rather than when you want him to. If you've adopted an older Schnauzer from a shelter, you can teach him all the rules of the house using the clicker. Once he understands that the click equals a treat, he'll be happy to oblige.

the most part, walking should be fun and easy. Unless you're doing obedience trials, it's not really necessary for your dog to maintain a strict heel at your side, but it's still important to teach him to walk nicely on a loose leash.

How to Teach Your Dog to Walk Nicely on a Leash

Put your dog on a leash using a flat buckle collar, and take him outside. When he pulls, stop in your tracks and wait for him to relax and for a little slack to come into the leash. The moment this happens, click and treat, then resume walking. Repeat this step until the dog realizes that if he pulls, he doesn't get anywhere, but if he relaxes, he will get a treat and continue walking. Once it's clear that he realizes what's going on, use the verbal cue "Let's go" as you continue walking. When he pulls toward another approaching dog or something else he wants, turn him around, walk in the other direction, and tell him firmly "Let's go." Then click and treat him for coming along.

The Mini Schnauzer is so intelligent and willing to please that training is actually a pleasure if you can find the right motivation for your dog. Fortunately, most Schnauzers will work for food or praise, so you have one less challenge right off the bat. Try not to get frustrated if your dog doesn't seem to be learning everything right away. Just keep at it, stay focused and positive, and remember to make training lessons fun for both of you.

Not only can your dog pulling on his leash be embarrassing, it's also dangerous, and it's just a lot more fun to walk a dog on a loose leash. Sure, he might pull when he sees another dog or something he wants to chase, but for

83

Being Good

Chapter 7

In the Doghouse

Schnauzer puppies are sweet and precious, but they aren't perfect forever. That adorable puppy you just brought home can wreck your furniture and your carpet, keep you up at night barking and whining, knock over the trash can, and generally make your life a lot more difficult than it was before he came along. This chapter will help you avoid or fix some of the behavioral issues that may drive you—and your neighbors—a little nuts.

Aggression

Many small dogs are allowed to be aggressive because they aren't seen as a real threat by their owners, but even a small aggressive dog can pose a serious danger to strangers, other animals, and family members.

Fortunately, this breed isn't known to be overly aggressive toward humans (although rodents are another story!), but any undersocialized dog can become fearful and aggressive if allowed to do so.

Solution

Never attempt to work with an aggressive dog on your own; this is a very serious problem that absolutely requires professional intervention. If you notice your dog exhibiting aggression toward humans—growling, baring teeth, snapping, or biting— consult a trainer or behaviorist right away. Dog-on-dog aggression is also dangerous and requires sessions with a trainer to correct.

Barking

Schnauzers are extremely territorial and will bark at just about any stimulus. It's in a dog's nature to bark, so some barking is normal and should be expected. For example, you should allow your Schnauzer a few barks to warn you of someone in the yard or at the door, but his barking

Excessive barking is common in Mini Schnauzers, who are naturally very vocal dogs.

shouldn't become so frequent that your neighbors start complaining.

Some dogs bark to excess because of separation anxiety, which can present itself as a set of destructive behaviors brought about by poor socialization or psychological trauma as a puppy, such as being left at a shelter after bonding to someone. If your Schnauzer barks nonstop when you leave the house and continues until you return, he probably has

Solution

Excessive barking is a difficult habit to break, especially with the Schnauzer, who is notorious for being a vigilant barker. Ideally, you can prevent barking by rewarding a puppy for quiet *sits* and *downs* and teaching him that being quiet earns him treats, but if the barking problem already exists, you'll have to come up with a training protocol to alter your dog's behavior.

Interrupting the barking cycle is the first tactic you should try: Shake a can full of pennies when your dog barks too many times. He will stop barking long enough to see what the racket is all about, giving you a chance to call him to you, give him a treat, and praise him for being quiet. If he gets a treat every time he stops barking, he'll eventually decide that barking isn't as much fun as eating or getting a pat on the head, and he'll come looking for you to hand out the goodies rather than barking like a maniac.

FAMILY-FRIENDLY TIP

Children and Aggressive Schnauzers

Aggressive Schnauzers are a danger to children even though they are small dogs. If your Schnauzer has shown aggression toward anyone, child or adult, consult a trainer or behaviorist right away. Schnauzers are generally wonderful family dogs, but an undersocialized Schnauzer who may have been taunted by children in the past is not going to trust children in the future.

If you have a child and an aggressive Schnauzer, keep the child and the dog separated until you can work with a trainer to resolve the issue. Instruct the child not to tease the dog or go near him when he's eating and to behave calmly when he is nearby. Often, running and screaming children can trigger aggression in a dog who is prone to this behavior.

Slow and Steady

When working with your dog to manage a problem behavior, you want him to be successful, so make the process easy for him. Don't let him get frustrated, and don't get frustrated yourself. Praise and reward your dog for small increments of progress toward a desired behavior, and don't expect too much too soon.

separation anxiety. If you don't know whether your dog barks all day while you're not around, ask your neighbors if they hear him, or leave a sound-activated recorder on while you're gone.

If your Schnauzer is barking because of separation anxiety, however, you have to work on that issue as the root of the problem to get the barking (and any related problem behaviors) to stop. Consult your veterinarian or a behaviorist if you suspect that your dog is suffering from separation anxiety.

Chewing

Most dogs think that chewing is a lot of fun, but puppies in particular chew to help their puppy teeth fall out and their adult teeth come in. Chewing feels good to them, and you're not going to be able to stop it, but you can direct a puppy to chew on acceptable things rather than your shoes or table legs. Adult dogs also like to chew but will quickly learn to chomp on the toys and treats you provide if you offer some great stuff.

Solution

Since you can't prevent your dog from chewing, the only thing you can do is offer him appropriate things to chew on and teach him what's inappropriate.

Provide your dog with plenty of suitable chew toys—for your sake as well as his!

Don't let your puppy chew on old sneakers, for example, because he won't be able to distinguish between the old ones and the new ones. Offer safe nylon or rubber toys as acceptable chews instead.

If your puppy does get ahold of something he shouldn't have, don't chase him. He'll think you're having fun playing "keep-away"—a puppy's favorite game—and he'll run away with the object. Instead of running after him, offer him a high-value treat or toy in exchange for the item he has and ask him to "leave it." When he drops your item and takes what you're offering, praise him and

If your Mini is a digger, protect your garden by offering him a safe, interesting place of his own in which to dig, such as a sandbox.

Solution

Try offering your Schnauzer his own sandbox filled with clean sand or soil. To get him interested in the box, bury balls, toys, and treats in the sand and encourage him to find them. He'll soon realize that digging in his own box is much more rewarding than digging in your garden. Place the box in a shady area and clean it often.

If you catch your dog digging somewhere he shouldn't, don't make a big deal about it. Call him to you, and reward him if he comes. If he doesn't come to you, walk calmly over to him and gently lead him away from the area by his collar. If he's still digging by the time you get to him, tell him "No!" in a firm, sharp voice. The harsh tone may stop the behavior, giving you a chance to redirect his energies.

Once you've moved him away from the hole he was digging, ask him to do something he knows how to do, like a *sit* or *down*, then praise and treat him for those behaviors. When he's in the yard by himself, give him something great to chew on to distract him, like

remove the object from his view. Eventually he'll learn that giving you objects results in him getting something even better.

Digging

Digging is a natural and fun activity for many dogs, especially terriers, but it's not great for your rhododendrons. Ruining the flowerbeds is only a small part of the problem, however—a dog who likes to dig can work his way under a fence and get hit by a car or lost.

a stuffed toy or a carrot smeared with peanut butter.

Inappropriate Elimination

Usually, accidents are the fault of inattentive owners. New puppies are going to have a housetraining accident here and there, especially if you aren't used to paying attention to your puppy's potty signals that tell you when he has to go out.

Sometimes a puppy will have a lapse in his housetraining, in which case you'll have to start the training process over from the beginning. However, if your formerly housetrained puppy is having a lot of accidents in the house, the issue might not be behavioral; he may have a bladder or kidney issue that requires veterinary attention.

Solution

To solve this problem, start your housetraining over again using praise and positive reinforcement. As long as the root of the problem is behavioral and not medical, positive reinforcement is a great way to get your Schnauzer to comply with the house rules.

Consider also that you may not be giving your Mini enough opportunities to potty outside. Puppies need to eliminate as many as eight times a day when they're young. Stick to a regular eating and walking schedule so that

The Expert Knows

Hiring a Behaviorist

If your Schnauzer continues to exhibit behaviors that baffle you or that you can't handle on your own, like aggression, consult an animal behaviorist or trainer who works with problem behaviors.

A good trainer or behaviorist will design a protocol based on your individual dog's issues. Look for someone who is compassionate and experienced both with the Schnauzer as a breed and with the specific issues your dog has. She should also use positive training methods and not advocate punishment as a means of correcting undesired behaviors. Finally, the behaviorist should make you comfortable enough to ask questions and try new things when training your dog.

your dog knows when he's going to get some time outside to do his thing. Also, use a natural deodorizer on the spot in the house where he has been eliminating. If the area still smells like urine or feces, he will be more likely to use that spot again.

Jumping Up

Jumping is definitely a common issue in Mini Schnauzers, but because they are small dogs, it's often an overlooked or accepted behavior. Dogs like to jump on people because they want to be closer to the person's face, where all the action is. Jumping isn't a terrible behavior in and of itself, but it can be pretty bad when a muddy dog jumps on your guest's white pants. Fortunately, jumping is a pretty easy problem behavior to solve in a Schnauzer.

Solution

Instead of touching your dog or talking to him when he jumps ("No, Schatzy, get down!"), ignore him and take a big step back until his four feet are on the floor before you greet him. Praise him for having "four on the floor," but look away and turn your back on him when he jumps, turning your attention immediately back to him when he's back on all fours. If your dog is still jumping up despite your ignoring him, say "Uh-uh" or "No" firmly as you back away, but don't allow the scolding to be the last word. Find something good to praise him for immediately after the incident.

Using the *sit* or *down* command is a perfect way to make a jumper behave himself. Train the *sit* or *down* so often that the behavior comes naturally for your dog—every time you have a treat in your hand, he should automatically sit. If he's sitting, he can't jump.

Self-rewarding behaviors like jumping are difficult to change, and your dog might go back to jumping even after you believe that you have gotten it under control. If your dog has a chronic jumping problem, put him on a leash and

Like many small dogs, Minis commonly jump up to get attention.

place your end of it under your foot. He will try to jump but won't be able to. Then, ask him for a *sit* or *down*, and treat him when he complies. Soon he'll learn that having four feet on the ground gets him attention and praise, which is what he wants.

Nipping/Play Biting

All puppies nip. They explore the world with their teeth and they nip during play, but those puppy teeth are sharp and can pierce your skin. Pups absolutely must learn that their teeth should never touch human skin. This is a critical lesson that you should begin as soon as you bring your puppy home for the first time.

Solution

To get your puppy to stop nipping, promote "kisses" instead. Spread a very thin layer of peanut butter on the back of your hands so that the puppy can lick it off. Praise highly

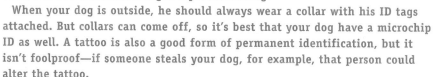

The Lost Dog

Finding a lost dog is easier today than ever before. Lost dog posters are effective, of course, but today we also have microchip identification, great dog ID tags and collars, and "Amber alert"-type notification systems that go out to dog owners in the area when a dog is reported missing.

When your dog is outside, he should always wear a collar with his ID tags attached. But collars can come off, so it's best that your dog have a microchip ID as well. A tattoo is also a good form of permanent identification, but it isn't foolproof—if someone steals your dog, for example, that person could alter the tattoo.

If your dog does become lost, look for him immediately, taking along as many people as you can find to help. Call him loudly and enthusiastically, shake a treat can, and squeak his favorite toy. If you can't find him right away, call all of the veterinarians and animal shelters in the area and tell them about your missing dog. Make a large fluorescent poster with your dog's photo or description, the word "reward" on it (but don't specify an amount), and a phone number (but not your address), and post it all over the neighborhood. Call breed rescue agencies in your area to tell them that you've lost a Schnauzer, and alert your microchip company immediately—they will often help you find your dog.

If you are unable to find your Mini, continue making phone calls and checking your local shelters every day. Hopefully a kind person will find him and bring him back to you.

Teaching Your Old Dog New Tricks

Older dogs respond very well to positive reinforcement training, especially clicker training, which is easy for a dog to understand when done properly. Undesirable behavior in older dogs usually stems from undersocialization and the lack of proper training. It's more difficult to train a behavior out of a dog than it is to train one into him, but trainers and dog owners do it every day.

Behavior substitution is a great way to get an older dog to change a behavior pattern. For example, if you don't want your dog to scratch at the door when he wants to go out, train him to ring a bell hanging from the doorknob instead.

Teach your dog from a young age that biting or nipping is never appropriate, even in play.

93

In the Doghouse

when he licks rather than nips, and offer treats for good behavior. If he nips, get up and walk away quietly. Don't make a fuss, eye contact, or punish him in any way. If the puppy nips at your ankles or pant leg, distract him with a toy and then praise him for playing with the toy.

Another way to prevent nipping is to use tactics that the puppy's mother and siblings would use. Show your dog a treat and then hold it in your closed fist. Offer him your fist, but if he nips, pull your hand back quickly and yelp loudly as another dog would do. Your puppy is programmed to understand that a yelp means that he's playing too roughly. Give him your hand again and repeat until your puppy gives a sniff or a kiss. Immediately offer the treat and praise him highly for his self-restraint.

Chapter 8

Stepping Out

A Schnauzer thrives on an active social life. Remember, he's small, but he's no delicate toy dog who needs to be carried everywhere. In fact, he's likely to enjoy a variety of sports, games, and other activities or just traveling to new places with his family. There are plenty of activities that will keep your dog entertained, and this chapter will give you some tips for traveling with your dog as well as an overview of games and sports in which both of you can participate.

Traveling With Your Schnauzer

Schnauzers like to be with their humans, so why not take yours along when you travel?

If you know exactly what to pack and what to expect, traveling with your dog can go very smoothly. But before you hit the road, you have to consider the joys and challenges of traveling with a dog.

Travel Preparations

Before you travel, get your dog ready by taking him to your veterinarian for an exam. Make sure that you get a health certificate and take it along with you, especially if you're leaving the country or traveling over state lines. If by some chance your dog falls ill during your journey, the certificate will save valuable time because it will show the animal hospital that your dog was well when he started the trip. Also, if there's an accident, first responders will need to assess your dog's situation and will be more likely to handle him nicely if they know that he has been vaccinated.

Finally, before you go, create or buy a doggy first-aid kit. (See Chapter 5 for tips on making your own kit.) Take it with you wherever you travel, and include your dog's health certificate, medical records, medicines, and contact phone numbers.

Lodging

Some hotels are very dog friendly and will welcome your dog with biscuits and a bed. Other hotels don't allow

Your Mini will enjoy traveling with you if you make the proper preparations.

Packing for Your Trip

When your Schnauzer is traveling with you, don't forget that you need to pack for him as well! Take the following items:

- your dog's paperwork showing that he's up to date on vaccinations
- appropriate identification tags, which should be kept on your dog at all times
- no-spill food and water bowls (no matter how you're traveling—car, train, ship, or plane—your dog will need food and water!)
- a pooper-scooper, plastic bags, and a deodorizing spray in case of any accidents
- your doggy first-aid kit
- a doggy sweater or coat (if it's cold where you're traveling)

dogs at all, however, so it's essential that you confirm all of your dog's accommodations before you leave. Also, ask about any extra pet fees or deposits, as well as the rules regarding where the dog is permitted to walk in the hotel.

It's best to bring a crate along in case your dog has to stay behind in the hotel room, especially because housekeeping staff will be entering your room and could let your dog out accidentally. (If you plan to take your dog out of the room with you, take a tote as well so that he can rest from walking or so that you can take him into a restaurant or other public place unnoticed.)

Airline Travel

If you're flying with your dog, find out all of the airline's guidelines and rules before your travel date. Airlines have rules about carriers and crates and will also need information about your dog's health before you fly.

Most Schnauzers are small enough to put under the seat or beneath your feet in an airline-approved tote bag. If your Schnauzer is too large for this, he may have to fly cargo, which comes with some real risks—he can become ill in the cargo hold, for example, or even lost. Also, be careful about traveling with your dog in cargo during extreme weather in the summer and winter.

Some airlines recommend that pets be sedated before being stowed on the plane, but you should discuss sedation with your veterinarian to get her recommendation. Sedation decreases a dog's oxygen intake and his reaction time, which can be dangerous in the event of an accident—for example, if workers accidentally dropped his crate. If sedation seems necessary for your dog to travel, consult your veterinarian about giving him a small amount of a sedative—enough to calm him down without knocking him out.

Car Travel

Puppies who are socialized early to riding in a car usually like it a lot by the time they grow up. They get to look out

97

With the proper introduction, your Mini can learn to love car travel.

the window, smell new scents, and go somewhere fun (hopefully not to the vet's office!). If your Schnauzer doesn't have much experience with car travel, get him used to the idea of a long car trip with a few practice runs that are meant to socialize him slowly to the idea of riding in the car.

Introducing Your Dog to the Car

Put your Schnauzer in the car and offer him treats, and then take him out again. Once he's okay with this, put him in the car and turn on the engine, then offer him treats and allow him out of the car. Repeat until he's happily jumping into the car on his own. Next, drive around for a few minutes, treating and praising him as you go, and then increase your driving time as your dog becomes comfortable with it. Then, choose a fun destination, like a park

FAMILY-FRIENDLY TIP

Traveling With Schnauzers and Children

Children and dogs can be a great match, but it's possible for kids to increase a dog's stress level while traveling by car. Make sure that the children are treating the dog nicely during the trip and aren't being rowdy near his crate or car seat. The dog should have an opportunity to relax and take a nap while you're on the road.

or dog run, and reward your dog with treats and playtime once you're there.

A Long and Winding Road

If you're going for a long road trip, bring along your dog's first-aid kit and a remedy for an upset stomach in case he gets carsick. (Your veterinarian can recommend a treatment for carsickness before the trip.) During the ride, make sure that your dog gets sufficient food and water at rest stops. Give him frequent bathroom breaks, and don't forget to bring plastic bags to clean up after him. You may also want to bring a deodorizing spray if he is prone to getting sick in the car.

Safety Concerns

Your dog should have some protection against injury in case of an accident while he's riding in the car. If your Schnauzer is used to a crate, put him inside and then buckle it in, using bungee cords to keep the crate in place. You can also purchase a dog harness or car seat that works with the seat belt to keep your dog from flying forward if you have to brake suddenly or if there's an accident. Also, dogs should *never* ride in the open bed of a pickup truck because they are vulnerable to inclement weather and debris that might blow off of other cars or trucks, and they might jump or be flung out in an accident.

When you leave the car, take your dog with you. Never leave him unattended in a car, even for a few minutes.

When He Can't Come With You

If you can't travel with your dog, you'll have to find someone who can take care of him while you're away. Asking a neighbor, family member, or friend is a great idea, but you may have to either board your dog in a kennel or locate a pet sitter if you can't find someone you know who will take the responsibility.

Dog Sitting

If you can't find a friend to pet sit your pooch, it's easy to find a professional pet sitter. The sitter you choose should

Make suitable arrangements for your dog's care if he can't travel with you.

SENIOR DOG TIP

Traveling With an Older Dog

Both an older pooch and a young dog need pretty much the same things when traveling: a safe kennel, food and water, moderate temperatures, and regular potty breaks. However, an older dog may need more potty breaks than a younger dog and might also need some help jumping in and out of the car. Also, long days of travel might be more stressful on the older dog. Keep these things in mind when planning to include an older pet on a trip.

be insured, experienced with pets, and have taken classes in pet first aid and CPR. Make sure that your sitter also has evacuation plans in case of a natural disaster.

Kenneling

If you have to kennel your dog while you're away, select your boarding facility the same way you'd choose a veterinarian. Go to the facility and ask to see where your dog will stay, and determine whether you're comfortable leaving him there.

Ask what paperwork the dog will need to be able to stay there—usually a health certificate showing certain vaccinations. Also, ask if there's a veterinarian on call and if she is available 24 hours a day.

Sports

Dog sports can be a blast for an active dog like the Mini Schnauzer. This breed often excels at sports that require beauty, grace, speed, and instinct. Here are just a few of the sports in which a Schnauzer has a good chance at bringing home a blue ribbon.

Agility

Agility trials are basically obstacle courses for dogs that include tasks such as jumping over bars, winding through poles, and running through tunnels. The aim is to have the dog finish the course in a specified amount of time, which requires that he be very smart and trainable—a perfect sport for the Mini Schnauzer, in other words. Agility trials are really fun to watch and even more fun to participate in, and they also provide fantastic exercise for both you and your pet.

Canine Freestyle

Canine freestyle is a dance competition for dogs and their owners. A song plays as the dog and owner go though a trained routine, kind of like canine ballroom dancing. It might sound a little unusual, but it's beautiful to watch, fun to participate in, and promotes bonding between you and your dog. Freestyle is also a great way to train your dog because he will have to know a variety of commands to perform a routine—and you'll both get a lot of exercise in the process.

Dog Shows (Conformation)

If your Schnauzer is registered with a kennel club, intact (not spayed or neutered), well socialized to other dogs and humans, properly trained, sound and healthy, and meets the breed standard for Schnauzers, he is eligible to compete in a conformation show. In this event, a judge evaluates participating dogs based on how well they conform to the breed standard.

Participating in conformation shows is a lot of fun, but it's also a lot of work. Fortunately, by getting involved in conformation, you'll meet a lot of other owners who are also passionate about the breed and possibly find a mentor to help you if you decide to show your dog.

Go to a couple of conformation shows before you consider entering your dog, and leave him at home when you go, as most shows don't allow unregistered dogs to enter the grounds.

Ground Trials

Schnauzers have been eligible to participate in earthdog trials since 1996. In an earthdog trial, a small animal such as a rat (the "quarry") is placed in a cage at the end of an underground tunnel. The dog must then "work" the quarry by digging, growling, barking, pawing, and otherwise trying to reach it. This is done to gauge the dog's hunting aptitude. It is a very controlled test, and neither the dog nor the quarry is harmed.

Agility is an excellent sport for the energetic Mini Schnauzer.

Obedience

Obedience trials require that a dog be extremely well trained and socialized to other dogs. Dogs participating in an obedience trial must successfully perform a variety of commands, some of which can be quite challenging. (Schnauzers are pretty good at obedience trials, but working and sporting breeds often trump them.)

Rally-O

Rally-o is like obedience but a little less formal. You and your Schnauzer will run from obstacle to obstacle and receive directions about which exercise to perform at each station. You are allowed to communicate as much as you please with your dog during this event, either vocally or through the use of hand gestures that indicate the behavior you want your dog to perform. Obedience trials are generally quieter and more formulaic, and they don't allow hand gestures.

Fun and Games

What if you don't want to get involved in organized sports? Although fun, they are also time consuming, and a lot of loving dog owners don't have that kind of time to spend. Fortunately, your Schnauzer will be just as thrilled with everyday activities that are closer to home, don't require

Sports and Safety

Dogs, like humans, need to ease their way into a workout. Before a Schnauzer begins training for a sport, he should have a physical to make sure that he's healthy. Also, speak with your vet about your dog's diet—with added exercise, your Schnauzer may need more food or different nutrients to compensate for all the energy he will burn.

When training your dog for a sport, begin slowly and gradually work him up to the level of exertion and ability the sport requires. Always start with a warm-up before practice or a competition, and make sure that your dog receives enough water throughout. During an outdoor competition, ensure that your dog is not too hot or cold and that he does not get too much sun.

much training, and best of all, can be done with you by his side.

Hide and Seek

Because Schnauzers are very people-oriented dogs, the game of hide-and-seek is perfect for them. While your dog is distracted (you can toss a treat or toy a few feet [meters] away to distract him), hide behind a door, or if you're outside, behind a tree. When he starts to look around to find you, pop out and call him enthusiastically, and give him a treat when he comes back. This is a great game to play with a puppy on a long leash—that way, if he starts to wander, you can always reel him in.

Hiking and Camping

Schnauzers are outdoorsy dogs who usually love to go on a nice hike or a camping trip with their humans. My Pepper loves romping through the brush, smelling all the wonderful scents, and when he goes out of sight I just call him back and he comes racing down the path back to me. He also runs up to other hikers, barking and "rooing," which sometimes scares people, so I often keep him on a retractable lead.

Many Miniature Schnauzers enjoy outdoor activities such as hiking or camping.

Packing for a Hike

Just as you'd bring water and a snack for yourself on a day of hiking, you have to bring supplies for your dog, too. Pack a bag for him that includes water and a foldable canvas bowl, a few treats (great for luring him back to you if he's chasing something), and tweezers in case he gets something stuck in his feet or nose. Don't forget flea and tick protection—whatever your veterinarian recommends. Also, when you get home from a hiking or camping trip, groom your dog, closely looking for ticks.

Sports and games can require a lot of effort, but they are absolutely worth your time. The degree of bonding and training you and your dog will get by participating in these activities are rewards well beyond a blue ribbon. Even if you don't want to participate in organized activities, a simple walk, hike, or game of fetch does wonders to expand your Schnauzer's horizons.

Resources

Associations and Organizations

Breed Clubs

American Kennel Club (AKC)
5580 Centerview Drive
Raleigh, NC 27606
Telephone: (919) 233-9767
Fax: (919) 233-3627
E-mail: info@akc.org
www.akc.org

Canadian Kennel Club (CKC)
89 Skyway Avenue, Suite 100
Etobicoke, Ontario M9W 6R4
Telephone: (416) 675-5511
Fax: (416) 675-6506
E-mail: information@ckc.ca
www.ckc.ca

**Federation Cynologique
Internationale (FCI)**
Secretariat General de la FCI
Place Albert 1er, 13
B – 6530 Thuin
Belqique
www.fci.be

The Kennel Club
1 Clarges Street
London
W1J 8AB
Telephone: 0870 606 6750
Fax: 0207 518 1058
www.the-kennel-club.org.uk

United Kennel Club (UKC)
100 E. Kilgore Road
Kalamazoo, MI 49002-5584
Telephone: (269) 343-9020
Fax: (269) 343-7037
E-mail: pbickell@ukcdogs.com
www.ukcdogs.com

Pet Sitters

**National Association of
Professional Pet Sitters**
15000 Commerce Parkway, Suite C
Mt. Laurel, New Jersey 08054
Telephone: (856) 439-0324
Fax: (856) 439-0525
E-mail: napps@ahint.com
www.petsitters.org

Pet Sitters International
201 East King Street
King, NC 27021-9161
Telephone: (336) 983-9222
Fax: (336) 983-5266
E-mail: info@petsit.com
www.petsit.com

Rescue Organizations and Animal Welfare Groups

**American Humane Association
(AHA)**
63 Inverness Drive East
Englewood, CO 80112
Telephone: (303) 792-9900
Fax: 792-5333
www.americanhumane.org

**American Society for the
Prevention of Cruelty to Animals
(ASPCA)**
424 E. 92nd Street
New York, NY 10128-6804
Telephone: (212) 876-7700
www.aspca.org

**Royal Society for the Prevention of
Cruelty to Animals (RSPCA)**
Telephone: 0870 3335 999
Fax: 0870 7530 284
www.rspca.org.uk

The Humane Society of the United States (HSUS)
2100 L Street, NW
Washington DC 20037
Telephone: (202) 452-1100
www.hsus.org

Sports
Canine Freestyle Federation, Inc.
Secretary: Brandy Clymire
E-Mail: secretary@canine-freestyle.org
www.canine-freestyle.org

International Agility Link (IAL)
Global Administrator: Steve Drinkwater
E-mail: yunde@powerup.au
www.agilityclick.com/~ial

North American Dog Agility Council
11522 South Hwy 3
Cataldo, ID 83810
www.nadac.com

North American Flyball Association
www.flyball.org
1400 West Devon Avenue #512
Chicago, IL 6066
800-318-6312

United States Dog Agility Association
P.O. Box 850955
Richardson, TX 75085-0955
Telephone: (972) 487-2200
www.usdaa.com

World Canine Freestyle Organization
P.O. Box 350122
Brooklyn, NY 11235-2525
Telephone: (718) 332-8336
www.worldcaninefreestyle.org

Therapy
Delta Society
875 124th Ave NE, Suite 101
Bellevue, WA 98005
Telephone: (425) 226-7357
Fax: (425) 235-1076
E-mail: info@deltasociety.org
www.deltasociety.org

Therapy Dogs Incorporated
PO Box 5868
Cheyenne, WY 82003
Telephone: (877) 843-7364
E-mail: therdog@sisna.com
www.therapydogs.com

Therapy Dogs International (TDI)
88 Bartley Road
Flanders, NJ 07836
Telephone: (973) 252-9800
Fax: (973) 252-7171
E-mail: tdi@gti.net
www.tdi-dog.org

Training
Association of Pet Dog Trainers (APDT)
150 Executive Center Drive Box 35
Greenville, SC 29615
Telephone: (800) PET-DOGS
Fax: (864) 331-0767
E-mail: information@apdt.com
www.apdt.com

National Association of Dog Obedience Instructors (NADOI)
PMB 369
729 Grapevine Hwy.
Hurst, TX 76054-2085
www.nadoi.org

Veterinary and Health Resources

Academy of Veterinary Homeopathy (AVH)

P.O. Box 9280
Wilmington, DE 19809
Telephone: (866) 652-1590
Fax: (866) 652-1590
E-mail: office@TheAVH.org
www.theavh.org

American Academy of Veterinary Acupuncture (AAVA)

100 Roscommon Drive, Suite 320
Middletown, CT 06457
Telephone: (860) 635-6300
Fax: (860) 635-6400
E-mail: office@aava.org
www.aava.org

American Animal Hospital Association (AAHA)

P.O. Box 150899
Denver, CO 80215-0899
Telephone: (303) 986-2800
Fax: (303) 986-1700
E-mail: info@aahanet.org
www.aahanet.org/index.cfm

American College of Veterinary Internal Medicine (ACVIM)

1997 Wadsworth Blvd., Suite A
Lakewood, CO 80214-5293
Telephone: (800) 245-9081
Fax: (303) 231-0880
Email: ACVIM@ACVIM.org
www.acvim.org

American College of Veterinary Ophthalmologists (ACVO)

P.O. Box 1311
Meridian, Idaho 83860
Telephone: (208) 466-7624
Fax: (208) 466-7693
E-mail: office@acvo.com
www.acvo.com

American Holistic Veterinary Medical Association (AHVMA)

2218 Old Emmorton Road
Bel Air, MD 21015
Telephone: (410) 569-0795
Fax: (410) 569-2346
E-mail: office@ahvma.org
www.ahvma.org

American Veterinary Medical Association (AVMA)

1931 North Meacham Road – Suite 100
Schaumburg, IL 60173
Telephone: (847) 925-8070
Fax: (847) 925-1329
E-mail: avmainfo@avma.org
www.avma.org

ASPCA Animal Poison Control Center

1717 South Philo Road, Suite 36
Urbana, IL 61802
Telephone: (888) 426-4435
www.aspca.org

British Veterinary Association (BVA)

7 Mansfield Street
London
W1G 9NQ
Telephone: 020 7636 6541
Fax: 020 7436 2970
E-mail: bvahq@bva.co.uk
www.bva.co.uk

Canine Eye Registration Foundation (CERF)
VMDB/CERF
1248 Lynn Hall
625 Harrison St.
Purdue University
West Lafayette, IN 47907-2026
Telephone: (765) 494-8179
E-mail: CERF@vmbd.org
www.vmdb.org

Orthopedic Foundation for Animals (OFA)
2300 NE Nifong Blvd
Columbus, Missouri 65201-3856
Telephone: (573) 442-0418
Fax: (573) 875-5073
Email: ofa@offa.org
www.offa.org

Publications

Books

Anderson, Teoti. *The Super Simple Guide to Housetraining*. Neptune City: TFH Publications, 2004.

DeGioia, Phyllis, *The Miniature Schnauzer*. Neptune City: TFH Publications, 2006.

Morgan, Diane. *Good Dogkeeping*. Neptune City: TFH Publications, 2005.

Magazines

AKC *Family Dog*
American Kennel Club
260 Madison Avenue
New York, NY 10016
Telephone: (800) 490-5675
E-mail: familydog@akc.org
www.akc.org/pubs/familydog

AKC *Gazette*
American Kennel Club
260 Madison Avenue
New York, NY 10016
Telephone: (800) 533-7323
E-mail: gazette@akc.org
www.akc.org/pubs/gazette

Dog & Kennel
Pet Publishing, Inc.
7-L Dundas Circle
Greensboro, NC 27407
Telephone: (336) 292-4272
Fax: (336) 292-4272
E-mail: info@petpublishing.com
www.dogandkennel.com

Dog Fancy
Subscription Department
P.O. Box 53264
Boulder, CO 80322-3264
Telephone: (800) 365-4421
E-mail: barkback@dogfancy.com
www.dogfancy.com

Dogs Monthly
Ascot House
High Street, Ascot,
Berkshire SL5 7JG
United Kingdom
Telephone: 0870 730 8433
Fax: 0870 730 8431
E-mail: admin@rtc-associates.freeserve.co.uk
www.corsini.co.uk/dogsmonthly

Resources

Index

Note: **Boldface** numbers indicate illustrations; an italic *t* indicates tables.

Index

Miniature Schnauzers

Index

Dedication

For Pepper and Ozzie, my tenacious, lovable, wonderful Miniature Schnauzers

About the Author

Nikki Moustaki, MA, MFA, is a dog trainer in New York City where she lives with her two Schnauzers. She is the author of several books on dogs and dog training, has written for many national magazines, and also writes extensively on bird care, training, and behavior. Nikki has been featured on television and radio shows and currently hosts www.dogfessions.com and www.dogvice.com.

Photo Credits

ANIMAL PLANET | ROAR
REACH OUT. ACT. RESPOND.